An ~~Un~~altered Life

BY PANCHO JUAREZ
and Jasmine Juarez

Church Contact Information

Calvary Chapel of Montebello
931 South Maple Avenue
Montebello, California 90640
(323) 724-8464
www.ccmtb.com

Scripture Quotations in this publication are from the
New International Version, Holman Bible Publishers

Dedication

P.J. : This book is dedicated to my best friend and beautiful wife, Millie.

J.J. : For my Dad, who never said no when asked to read an extra chapter at bedtime.

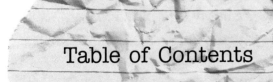

Table of Contents

Forward

As I sit at my desk to begin writing this book, I cannot help but begin sorting out my thoughts and feelings. The one image that quickly flashes through my mind is that of my two year old daughter standing behind our old rickety screen door frantically waving her pudgy-fingered starfish hand every day when I arrived home from work. She would push and pound on that screen door, until I finally opened it and lifted her up so that she could bury her head in my neck with her usual enthusiasm that never failed to melt my heart.

I wonder where those days have passed. Even though my daughter still finds a way to bury her head in my neck 23 years later, she has found another man to hold her in his arms. My oldest daughter, Jasmine, is getting married to a wonderful young man and though she talks to me nonstop about the catering, centerpieces and photography, I can only think of how my life has changed. God has brought me incredibly far from my desperate days of youth to a place of paternal joy and pride.

I emigrated to the United States when I was about 11 years old and it is without a doubt that I can say, truly, God had His hand on me while I struggled growing up in the concrete mazes of East Los Angeles. I remember the first day of school when the teacher couldn't say Francisco Alejandro Gomez-Juarez correctly and had to shorten it to Francis Juarez. Unbeknownst to my freshly immigrated self, there was a television show that starred a mule named Francis. The entire class hee-hawed my name for the next few days and I couldn't determine whether American children made donkey sounds for pleasure or spite as part of their salutations. When I realized that the kids were making fun of me, I immediately told my teacher—in broken English—to call me Frank, after the only American singer I knew, Frank Sinatra.

I made friends and assimilated quickly, but my life drifted along a crooked path. It wasn't until I accepted Jesus Christ as my Lord and Savior that I knew what it meant to have a real friend, someone who cared so much for me that He willingly took my sins as His own. For the first time in my life, I found a friend that didn't have the capacity to rank out; a friend who never left my side when the going got tough; a friend that stayed by my side, no matter how badly I treated Him. Never once had anyone taken the rap for me. Once I acknowledged that I needed

Jesus Christ more than He needed me, and that my life was impotent without God, He began to use me for His kingdom.

I never dreamed the day would come so soon when I would be giving away my daughter on her wedding day. As I begin the journey of writing this book with her help and encouragement, I realize that I have nothing that hasn't been given to me by God. May this book serve as a testament of God's omnipotent power and sovereignty. My testimony isn't spectacular or extraordinary, but my goal is to paint a picture of my life in order to show that God can do amazing things. I am but one man being used for the glory and edification of our Lord and Savior Jesus Christ.

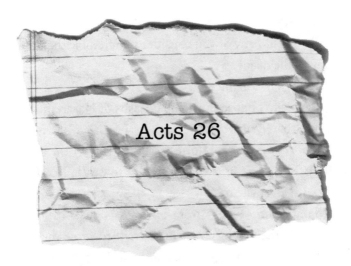

Acts 26

1. Then Agrippa said to Paul, "You have permission to speak for yourself." So Paul motioned with his hand and began his defense:

2. "King Agrippa, I consider myself fortunate to stand before you today as I make my defense against all the accusations of the Jews,

3. and especially so because you are so well acquainted with all the Jewish customs and controversies. Therefore, I beg you to listen to me patiently

4. "The Jews all know the way I have lived ever since I was a child, from the beginning of my life in my own country, and also in Jerusalem.

5. They have known me for a long time and can testify, if they are willing, that according to the strictest sect of our religion, I lived as a Pharisee.

6. And now that it is because of my hope in what God has promised out fathers that I am on trial today.

7. This is the promise our twelve tribes are hoping to see fulfilled as they earnestly serve God day and night. O King, it is because of this hope that the Jews are

accusing me.

8. Why should any of you consider it incredible that God raises the dead?

9. "I too was convinced that I ought to do all that was possible to oppose the name of Jesus of Nazareth.

10. And that is just what I did in Jerusalem. On the authority of the chief priests I put many of the saints in prison, and when they were put to death, I cast my vote against them.

11. Many a time I went from one synagogue to another to have them punished, and I tried to force them to blaspheme. In my obsession against them, I even went to foreign cities to persecute them.

12. "On one of these journeys, I was going to Damascus with the authority and commission of the chief priests.

13. About noon, O king, as I was on the road, I saw a light from Heaven, brighter than the sun, blazing around me and my companions.

14. We all fell to the ground, and I heard a voice in Aramaic, 'Saul, Saul, why do you persecute me? It is hard for you to kick against the goads.'

15. "Then I asked, 'Who are you, Lord?' 'I am Jesus who you are persecuting,' the Lord replied.

16. 'Now get up and stand on your feet. I have appeared to you to appoint you as a servant and as a witness of what you have seen of and what I will show you.

17. I will rescue you from your own people and from the Gentiles. I am sending you to them

18. to open their eyes and turn them from darkness to light, and from the power of Satan to God, so that they may receive forgiveness of sins and a place among those

who are sanctified by faith in me.'

19. "So then, King Agrippa, I was not disobedient to the vision from Heaven.

20. First to those in Damascus, then to those in Jerusalem and in all Judea, and to the Gentiles also, I preached that they should repent and turn to God and prove their repentance by their deeds.

21. That is why the Jews seized me in the temple courts and tried to kill me.

22. But I have had God's help to this very day, and so I stand here and testify to small and great alike. I am saying nothing beyond what the prophets and Moses said would happen—

23. that the Christ would suffer and, as the first to rise from the dead, would proclaim light to his own people and to the Gentiles."

24. At this point Festus interrupted Paul's defense. "You are out of your mind, Paul!" he shouted. "Your great learning is driving you insane."

25. "I am not insane, most excellent Festus," Paul replied. What I am saying is true and reasonable. The king is familiar with these things, and I can speak freely to him. I am convinced that none of this has escaped his noticed, because it was not done in a corner. King Agrippa, do you believe the prophets? I know you do."

26. Then Agrippa said to Paul, "Do you think that in such a short time you can persuade me to be a Christian?"

27. Paul replied, "Short time or long—I pray God that not only you but all who are listening to me today may become what I am, except for these chains.

Introduction

One of my most vivid memories during my first trip to Israel was when I visited the amphitheater in Caesarea, where Paul testified in front of Agrippa. Having committed Acts 26 to heart, there came a moment during my visit when I felt Paul's words haunting me. When everyone on the tour left the amphitheater to take pictures by the seaside, I was moved to walk down to the center floor and was able to listen to the echo of my voice after I spoke a few words. Next thing I knew, I began reciting Acts 26 aloud. With my feet firmly planted on the caramel-colored marble, I passionately said, "I am not insane, most noble Festus!" Just then, a few people came back into the amphitheater. I immediately stopped my monologue, but they urged me to keep going. I politely declined not out of embarrassment, but by sheer virtue of the fact that I was caught up in emotion. I pictured Paul insisting that he was sane—

he knew the transformation that occurred on the road to Damascus and he knew of the changes that took place in his life. Paul stood in front of very powerful men insisting that he was not a lunatic, and whether they believed it or not, everything happened the way he claimed. In the same vein, I want to take this opportunity to write about things that have happened in my life; things that have molded me into the man I am today and I want to assure the reader that I am not crazy, despite what my wife and children might say! I acknowledge, however, that perhaps I am crazy, crazy in love with my Lord and Savior, Jesus Christ!

I gave my life to Christ about 30 years ago. But, allow me to go back further in time to moments that defined my desperate need for God; experiences that led me to *needing* Him. You see, in the course of living, there are events, or—as many refer to them— defining moments that shape our character. These moments dictate who we are and who we eventually become. Dysfunctional family dynamics, sexual and domestic abuse, poverty and racism—these are just a handful of traumatic events that one can reflect on, as an adult, and recognize the long-term psychological damage. Things happen in this wicked world. There are some people who get to a place in their lives without Jesus Christ and realize there is a vacuum inside their soul, a seemingly empty void. This is what happened to me in May 1975, but it would be best for me to start at the beginning and work up to this point. I've broken my story from this point into five distinct segments, or *phases*, coinciding with five life-altering milestones.

In 1969, I joined the United States Marine Corps. This was the first milestone in my young life. The Marine Corps told me what to do, how to do it, when to get up, when to go to sleep, when to eat, when to shower—the Pentagon gave me orders and I followed them, no questions asked. The regimen and the discipline I received from the Corps altered my life in unthinkable ways.

In 1975, my life changed again and this change had the most dramatic impact—I became a Christian and dedicated my life to Christ. The next significant alteration came when I married my wife, Millie. Marriage alters you; there's a reason why people are married at the *altar*! For those of you who have been married less than a year, you might read this and wonder what I'm talking about. Well, just wait and see. Right now, you're in the Disneyland mode of walking down Main Street, but once the first year passes, you'll discover that Disneyland is also known for its crazy rollercoasters!

In 1980, my life changed yet again when my wife and I became parents for the first time to not only one, but *two* babies! Now, this was a major alteration because, quite frankly, I didn't know the slightest thing about being a father.

The fifth, and final, defining moment of my life came about five years ago when Millie was diagnosed with two forms of cancer. This episode changed everything. The man I was, and the man I wanted to become, forever changed as a result of Millie's illness.

For this reason, I am shackled to God's all mighty power.

You most likely have alterations that are much different from mine. Life events materialize in a variety of experiences. Perhaps you lost your mom or dad at a young age, tragically lost a sibling, or had to raise a family before reaching adulthood. Such factors may lead to the loss of innocence and may cause life-long wounds. While your story may be different than mine, it is my hope that you find shades of yourself in these pages. It is in these commonalities that we can find the familiar thread that ties us together as we follow the upward calling of God.

Camino de Guanajuato

"No vale nada la vida.
La vida no vale nada.
Comienza siempre llorando y asi llorando se acaba.
Por esto es que en este mundo la vida no vale nada"

JOSE ALFREDO JIMENEZ

I was born in 1952—the youngest of three—in the colonial town of San Miguel de Allende, Guanajuato, Mexico. My father was an alcoholic, an abusive husband and a womanizer. He was absent most of the time, so I have vague memories of him. What little I do remember, however, is that he abused my mother emotionally, psychologically and physically.

There is a part of me that thinks my father tried to be a family man. But, the man could not function without being intoxicated. It was his dependence on alcohol, and his unquenchable thirst for it, that led to the breakdown of my family. My father followed a strict regimen of drinking into belligerence, beating my mother mercilessly, stealing items from our home to fund his sexual escapades and then disappearing for five months at a time. He would then return sober and swear to make things better. My mother—with her hopes and dreams rooted in his empty words—took him back every time.

During this chaotic period, my mother owned a little eatery—an *Orange Julius* type of stand—and made just enough money to provide a stable lifestyle. At this time, while my mother served as the sole breadwinner, my father began to have an affair with a married woman in our small town. When the adulteress' husband discovered the truth, he threatened to kill my father if he remained in town, so my father immediately left my family—and my mother's hopes and dreams—by the wayside. Little did I realize this would be the last time I'd ever see him. I was seven years old.

Abandoned to care for three children, my mother was left emotionally vulnerable for anyone to come in and sweep her off her feet. And that's what happened with a man 10 years her junior.

Several years after my father's hasty departure, a young soccer player moved to town and became a boarder in one of the rooms my mother rented. Popular on the soccer field, he was even more popular with the women in town. He was a sweet-talker and tickled my mother's ears with candied words and big promises. This haphazard Casanova knotted my mother's stomach, melted her heart and fathered a child with her shortly thereafter.

While I dribbled my soccer ball through cobblestoned streets on my way to the bullfights, my mother was having an affair with her new lover. Shortly thereafter, the townspeople began whispering about her swollen belly and soon after about the birth of my sister. My sister, Blanca, was barely a year old when my mother's boyfriend fled north to the United States. Once again, my mother was left alone.

In 1959, my mother packed our bags and moved us to the Mexican/American border with hopes of beginning her business again. My family was penniless after my mother's boyfriend left because our neighbors boycotted my mother's shop on account of her illegitimate child. Her business plummeted and that forced my siblings and me to get any job we could. My mother was labeled a floozy and backs turned against us, so she decided to move and begin anew with help from her sister, Socorro.

My mother moved us into the Twilight Zone— the gates of Hell if you will—more commonly known as Tijuana, Mexico. I was eight years old.

I remember asking very pointedly why we had to move and having my questions quickly dismissed. Living in Tijuana was a surreal experience. The sheer ugliness of the city gave me the certainty that I wouldn't settle into this lifestyle. Afterall, I moved from a beautiful town with all the amenities of a home, to a city where water was only available on certain days of the week and an outhouse was the closest thing to a bathroom.

Uprooted unexpectedly from a happy and secure home, we hopped from place to place for a year. It was more than I could bear. My life finally regained stability when my mother procured a home in Tijuana and I began to attend school regularly. But my security was shattered once again when my mother's boyfriend tracked her down. He was living in Miami, Florida and said he'd be moving to Los Angeles, the city of dreams. His sweet words and silver tongue convinced my mother that he was sorry for abandoning us. So, she worked toward saving enough money to get us across the border. "If God wills it," she said, "we'll get there."

Looking back at my religious upbringing, I was raised in a Roman Catholic home, but Catholicism was never practiced. Although my military dog-tags are imprinted with *Roman Catholic*, I never knew what it meant to be religious. My experience was such that my Catholic family never read the Bible and hardly even knew it existed.

When my family moved into our own home, the first thing I wanted to do was my First Holy Communion. Once we had a permanent place to live, I found a church to call my own and enrolled in the First Holy Communion workshop. Looking back, it was sheer lunacy. I wanted to go through this whole process of Catechism and First Holy Communion only because my friends had already completed their communions and teased me relentlessly for not following suit. They taunted me and asked me where I would go if I died. I didn't want to go to Hell, so I began to attend church on my own. The peer pressure was so strong that I took Catechism classes just to prove that I wasn't damned to Hell. I was going to prove it by dressing up and lighting my candle. During my last Catechism class—just days before my First Holy Communion was to take place—news of the Cuban Missile Crisis broke and Nikita Khrushchev threatened to bomb the United States. President Kennedy stood his ground. As a result, Mexicans in Tijuana feared that the U.S. naval base in San Diego, California was a prime target. Mexicans moved south in droves, so as to avoid the effects of a nuclear attack. This sudden southern migration caused hysteria and left many Mexicans wondering where to go. In hindsight, even if all Mexicans moved to the southern most tip of Baja California, they would not have escaped the effects of a nuclear attack. Either way, with America's focus on Cuba, the Mexican/American border became lax making it easier for my family to enter United States. So, in 1963, we were on the move once again.

Our Day Will Come

"Our day will come if we just wait a while no tears
  for us.
Think love and wear a smile.
Our dreams have magic because we'll always be in
  love this way.
Our day will come."

RUBY AND THE ROMANTICS

My mother packed all of our belongings into two tattered bags that she balanced on her tired shoulders as we boarded the Greyhound bus bound for Los Angeles. I pressed my forehead against the bus window and cried quietly. I cried for my older brother and sister who were to remain in Tijuana until my mother was able to make arrangements for them to join us. I cried fearing that immigration officers—*la migra*—would see through my mother's lie when she presented the 72-hour passports she had secured for herself, my baby sister and me. I cried because we were going to live in Los Angeles illegally with my mother's boyfriend, and because I was going to have to start a new life in a foreign country.

My mother married her boyfriend immediately after we arrived, making my young life more difficult as I adapted to having a new stepfather. Just like the mismatched furniture, he became a permanent fixture in our home. We lived in a small house on 15th and Maple in Downtown Los Angeles; a house so small, that if you wanted to change your mind, you had to go outside. Needless to say, music soon became my outlet and a way to escape the confines of such small living quarters. I often crawled into bed, laid next to my transistor radio, and escaped the thin walls of my home and the swirling noise outside my door.

My family listened to the Spanish station, but I listened to stations playing the latest 1960s hits, among them KFWB (it wasn't an all-news station back then). I loved R&B, but if I wanted to be really cool, I'd listen to smooth jams on KJLH. And, if I wanted to get down and funky, I'd tune into KGFJ and listen to one of my favorite disc-jockeys, *Magnificent Montague*!

I didn't realize it at the time, but listening to this music caused me to become culturally detached from my family. This eventually led to a very distinct division between me and my mother and siblings as I pulled away. While they listened to songs of heartache and woe from our motherland, I longed for the smooth sounds of Otis Redding and Wilson Pickett.

I think part of the reason that I let music kidnap my mind was because I couldn't stand my home life.

My friends Otis and Wilson would drown out the sounds of my stepfather arguing with my mother; rhythmic waves of beats and lyrics soothed me, making me think, *Everything will be okay.*

My stepfather, like my father, was a womanizer. I can still see the chronic look of desperation on my mother's face. While she tried masking her unhappiness with mascara and lipstick, the anguish wore on longer than her make-up. She fashioned a look of exasperation as she relived the trauma and heartbreak first caused by my father.

When my father cheated on my mother, I was young and without a voice. When he beat my mother, I was powerless and cowered in a corner. I kept silent and wished the earth would freeze on its axis, pausing just long enough for my mother to escape. In Los Angeles, once again I heard the barbed noises of fighting and physical altercations. This time, unlike the many times before, I was old enough to stand up for my mother. But, when I tried to fight on her behalf, she sacrificed herself rather than see me hurt and instead locked herself with my stepfather in their bedroom to absorb the blows behind closed doors.

To escape the chaos of our small house, I spent a lot of time watching television. I was the first in my family to learn English. With the help of American sitcoms, it took me less than six months! So, quite naturally, and out of necessity, I became the mouthpiece for everything—from grocery shopping to trips to the doctor—a sort of *Pocahontas*, if you will. I accompanied my mother everywhere as an interpreter and, because of this, I missed school for two years. Two years! When I wasn't out with my mother, I stayed home and studied American culture through the powerful medium of 1960s television. I quickly became familiar with the ever popular *Ozzie and Harriet, Johnny Yuma* and the *Flintstones*. When I watched *Ozzie and Harriet,* I'd laugh out loud, but my laughter was often interrupted because I had to interpret the show for my family. I had to explain to my mother why Harriet wore elegant dresses while she cooked dinner and why she never served tortillas. Needless to say, the show wasn't as funny in Spanish, so I would often pretend not to understand what was said so as to avoid another interpretation.

Television preoccupied most of my time as a kid. However, on occasion, my mother and stepfather took my siblings and me to the Spanish drive-in theater, the Floral Drive-In (which I still hate with a passion). This was of particular disinterest to me as a young boy because there were a lot of *homeboys* from the Maravilla projects. I first heard about the Maravillas while I took a beating at the drive-in. As I got older, the homeboys started asking me, "Where you from?" At the time I had no clue what this talk was about; I was innocent. Later, I would find out that it was a question, and a threat, regarding what gang I was with. This marked the beginning of my problems.

I was bicultural and bilingual and—basically—messed up. I wondered, *What am I?* and I walked a fine line between two different worlds; neither of which allowed me to define who I was. In my 11-year-old mind, I was an English-speaking American one second, and a Spanish-speaking Mexican the next. I couldn't find a balance between the country of my birth and the country that had adopted me. I thought of myself as no longer being truly Mexican, but not yet fully American either. This became apparent as I carried my homemade bean burritos to school inside my Flintstone's lunchbox.

Prisoner of Love

"Alone from night to night you'll find me.
Too weak to break the chains that bind me.
* I need no shackles to remind me. I'm just a*
* prisoner of love.*
I can't escape for it's too late now, I'm just a prisoner
* of love."*

JAMES BROWN

I suppose one can say that my adult life began in 1964, when I was just 12 years old. I call this year the *rape of innocence*. Things happened to me in my childhood that I was never able to tell anyone. When these things happened, I kept my mouth shut and locked up these events in my young heart. It wasn't until I met my wife that I was able to share my darkest secrets. I divulged pieces of my inner world to her and also to Jesus Christ. It was only then when I felt true liberation from within.

The violation of innocence I experienced was a *moral abuse,* as John Nieder describes in his book *God, Sex and Your Child.* Nieder writes:

Moral abuse is the violation of a child's innocence which occurs when a child is exposed to sexual information that he cannot comprehend or that overwhelms his moral defenses.

When a child sees something pornographic, or any kind of sexual perversity, his moral defense mechanism (i.e. his conscience) is not built up yet and, therefore, cannot properly process the images.

Pornographic material was shown to me as a child by a 20-year-old woman. This woman was exotic and intriguing to me when I was 12 years old. In hindsight, I can see that she was sexually active and the product of a dysfunctional and broken family. But, I didn't see any of this back then. All I knew was that she was *fine* and I instantly became attracted to her because she made me feel good. At my young age, I thought that she shook my heart, but what she really did was titillate my loins. And what began as the sexual curiosity of a young boy eventually led to my physical seduction.

Bad things happen when kids are left alone. Children cannot discern between good and evil—that's what parents are for. When children get caught up in trouble, it's hard to get them out. I found myself drawn back to this seductive woman again and again the same way a drug addict searches for another hit. All I wanted was to feel loved. My heart was broken when I realized that I wasn't the only one paying visits to this woman. Many of my friends were doing the same thing. And, the perversion became weirder and weirder as she manipulated the fragile situation to her advantage. For many years, I kept hidden the sexual experimentation that occurred when I was 12 years old. I was ashamed of it. Years later, this sexual distortion caused me to always keep my children within yelling distance. Till this day, whenever I'm looking for any of my five children, all I have to do is give the family whistle, and my grown children still respond.

For many years after, I felt shameful of everything that happened in my childhood. It wasn't until I read Tim Le Haye's book, *The Unhappy Gay*, that I was able to break free from my childhood shackles. When fatherless boys are left alone for long periods of time, writes Le Haye, they don't have proper knowledge about sex. Young boys have a sexual drive and if there is no one to properly instruct them regarding this subject, they will turn to secondhand information (or experimentation) to learn about sexuality. I always stress that it is the father's responsibility to instruct their sons about sex. I felt stigmatized by my childhood experience because it went against my conscience, my moral fiber. Young and naïve, my moral defenses were weak and I was unable to intellectually digest what was happening to me.

Looking back today, I can tell you how horrible this experience was, but as a youngster in 1964, I'd tell you it wasn't so bad. In fact, our encounters felt sinfully good. My seductress turned something pure—something God created—into something intoxicatingly bad. I found myself going back to her like a magnet to gratify the same erotic feelings again. The most destructive part of this activity was that it was done in secret. Having lacked a father or a full parental unit, I wanted this woman to provide something I desperately needed—love.

My mother was a hard-working woman and the only one who held a steady job. Every morning, she rode the bus Downtown to earn a living as a sweatshop worker. This meant I was left unsupervised most of the day. To keep my mom from worrying about me, I convinced her I was capable of staying home alone, so I didn't allow her to leave lunch for me; I told her I was old enough to make my own.

Everyday I walked down to a corner store and bought *Fritos*, deviled ham and an *RC Cola*. I would plop on the couch and dip, crunch and slurp my way into my favorite meal of the day. My mother hated my awful lunch concoction, so she made me breakfast every morning. Although her meals were delicious, I couldn't wait for lunch to roll around because I would dutifully bring out my *Fritos* and salsa. On these long afternoons, I glued myself to the television and watched *I Love Lucy* and *The Andy Griffith Show*. Mesmerized by these shows, I watched them religiously during hours that I should have spent in a classroom.

Often, people wonder why I wasn't enrolled in school, but—to be honest—besides having to interpret for my mother, I didn't go to school because my mother did not know how to matriculate me into the American school system. Her lack of knowledge kept me home and out of school for almost two years.

A Change is Gonna Come

"It's been too hard living
But I'm afraid to die 'cause I don't know what's out
there beyond the sky.
It's been a long, a long time coming.
But I know a change is gonna come."

SAM COOKE

In 1965, my life finally began to take the shape of something normal. I was enrolled at 28th Street School in South Los Angeles. As the *Four Tops* released a hit called *Ask the Lonely,* I began the fifth grade and I felt good because I was advanced in Geography, World History and Math. The only problem I faced was that I hadn't mastered the English language. English speaking or not, I advanced to the sixth grade and graduated from elementary school.

I recall two teachers who made a huge impact on

my life: Mr. Wilson and Mrs. Edwards. Both African-Americans, they showered me with encouragement, hugs, and pats on the back that gave me inspiration to pursue my education. If I had the opportunity to talk to them today, I would thank them from the bottom of my heart. Teachers, especially the few I speak of in this book, made the biggest difference in my life and helped mold me into the man I am today. I remain indebted to their kindness when I couldn't find the right English words to say and I am grateful for their patience and instruction, which ultimately helped me form my thoughts.

In 1966, I enrolled in John Adams Junior High School in South Los Angeles. I continued to earn excellent grades (again thanks to wonderful teachers), but, once again, I had to move in 1967. My family moved further into South Los Angeles, near the intersection of Figueroa and Jefferson (where the *Felix the Cat* Chevrolet dealer is located), close to the University of Southern California (USC). What made this move so appealing to me was that we also lived close to the Shrine Auditorium, which was used for major concerts. I got to see Jimi Hendrix, The Doors, Jefferson Airplane, Hugh Masekela, Janis Joplin and many others.

Okay, I have to take this moment to talk about Jimi Hendrix. You know, not only am I a Christian, I am also a pastor. I asked the Lord to take away the love I have for Jimi Hendrix's music. I've literally begged God to take Jimi out of my thoughts because the moment I listen to his music, my head begins to involuntarily move back and forth. I am over 50 years old, I wear bifocals, I have no hair, but when I hear the familiar sounds of *Tu Tu Tum, Tum, Foxy Lady*...wow! It's as if I'm taken to another point in time and, although I've asked the Lord to take this away from me, the feeling still remains. I was only 14 when I started going to these events at the Shrine. Concerts where people were sometimes nude or simply going crazy, strung out on psychedelic acid (LSD) and mescaline. It was during this era that I began dealing and using drugs, which began with marijuana.

I remember the acid trips during my times at the Shrine, the mescaline with the weed, and all the drinking I did. I remember the cheap wines of yesteryear: *Ripple, Bali Hi, Santa Fe Port Wine* and, when I had no money, some horrible liquor called *Short Dogs*. If you don't know what this is, then God bless you! This liquor was terrible and it was the first indication that I was turning into a drunk.

My friends and I would get loaded and head to the Shrine with no money. We would then rush the gates—in a group of 15 guys or so—to get in. With only two security guards at the gate, they were only able to stop two or three of us. And, of course, I always ensured that I was in the middle of the pack.

Some people ask how I was able to get away with everything, but it was easy because I never had to check in at home. My mother was so busy and fatigued that I was often on the streets until 1 or 2 a.m. To fund my escapades, I went onto the USC campus and stole bicycles. I would steal a bike when

I needed to get home and then sell it for $5 to a kid in the neighborhood. When I needed more money, off to USC I went to steal another bike.

My friends tried telling me that I was a thief, but I argued that with so many bikes, one missing bike wouldn't make a difference. Besides, I told myself, I was providing a service for the disadvantaged children of South Los Angeles. Where else would they find such a good price for a bike? I saw myself as a modern day Robin Hood, minus the tights. During the summer, when I knew that many students were leaving their dorms and graduating, I would go on a bicycle *shopping spree* of sorts. It seemed like everyday I was riding a new bike home. If you went to USC in 1967 and you're bike was stolen, I'm sorry.

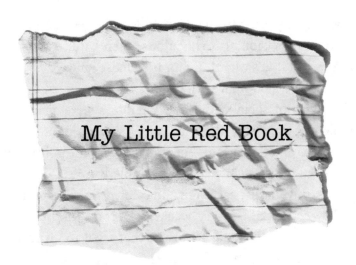

My Little Red Book

*"I just got out my little red book the minute that you
said goodbye.*
I thumbed right through my little red book.
I wasn't gonna sit and cry.
And I went from A to Z.
I took out every pretty girl in town.
*They danced with me and as I held them all I did was
talk about you.*
Hear your name and I'd start to cry.
There's just no getting over you."

L<small>OVE</small>

Something else was going on in my life besides
bicycle thievery at this time. I was about 15 years old
when I began riding my bike to Venice Beach. I would
ride the 13 miles to Venice because Mike Blodgett,
a popular TV personality, did a live television show
there at 6 p.m. called *Groovy*. I would leave my house
at noon and ride my bike those many, many miles just

to swing my arms from side to side in hopes of being seen on television. It's ridiculous when I think about it now, but that's what I did for fun. I also enjoyed *love-in* gatherings popular with hippies that promoted love as a form of social activism. Attendees were against violence, especially the Vietnam War, and embraced the notion of freedom—personal freedom, political freedom and sexual freedom. People wore tie-dye t-shirts, waved the peace sign and carried signs that said "Flower Power." Every weekend, I rode the bus or hopped in a stolen car to ensure that I got to Griffith Park in time for these festivities.

In 1967, I was at a *love-in* at Griffith Park where I had every drug made available to me for free. Everything was free. Free mescaline, acid, *reds*, *whites*, beer, wine, free peanut butter and jelly sandwiches, for crying out loud! But it did not stop with illegal drug use, as people performed sexual acts in front of my eyes. I was only 15 years old and the notion of sexual freedom further distorted my view of sex, amplifying the existing perversity.

During this time, I became sexually promiscuous with girls who—in hindsight—were also from broken homes or dysfunctional families. I was 15 and it was open-season on girls; they were easy targets. These girls often came from homes like mine where there was no supervision for lack of a father or as the result of an overworked mother. There was no parent or guardian to ask the questions that parents should ask.

Someone should have asked me where I was going, with whom I was going and what time I would return. But no one asked. I would spend the day at the beach getting loaded and would then crawl into the backseat of a car with a girl who lived a life equal to mine.

White Rabbit

"One pill makes you larger and one pill makes you
  small
And the ones that mother gives you don't do anything
  at all
Go ask Alice when she's ten feet tall."

JEFFERSON AIRPLANE

In 1967, I was to attend Jefferson High School in South Los Angeles, a school with a student body almost entirely African-American. On my first day of school, I was jumped by two different gangs, the *Outlaws* and the *Business Men,* when I couldn't answer which gang I belonged to. They asked, "Where you from? Clanton? The Flats?" When I answered "No" to every question, they asked again, "Well, where you from?!" "Mexico," I finally replied. That's when I got jumped again.

I couldn't identify with anyone in school. I wasn't

Black, so I wasn't accepted in African-American gangs. The *cholos* (hard core Mexican gangsters) didn't accept me either because, quite frankly, I was a lover and not a fighter. Worst of all, I wasn't even accepted by the *pochos* (Mexican-Americans who are fully acclimated to American culture and usually don't speak Spanish) because I wasn't one of them either. I was the odd man out, which meant I was constantly being jumped. Having to deal with these questions and problems at 15 years old was difficult and intensified the questions I had about my cultural identity.

Because I was beaten at almost every corner, my mother transferred me to a different high school. I went to Roosevelt High School, but I didn't live in East Los Angeles. So, I used a phony address on Estrada Courts off Olympic Boulevard. My transfer paperwork was completed and accepted and off I went to Roosevelt High.

When I began at Roosevelt, I held two jobs. I worked at *Woody's Smorgasburgers* by the USC campus, and at the first East Los Angeles *Jack in the Box* off Mott Street and Brooklyn Avenue. *Jack in the Box* was literally in the shape of a box. I was one of the first employees to open this restaurant and I was proud to work there. I started as the french fry and drink man, but hated wearing the white paper hat, so I became the grill man. Being the grill man was the equivalent to being a demigod in the fast food restaurant world. I no longer wore the white paper hat, but proudly wore a *red* hat. This was big stuff! There was no where else to move but up on Jack's employment ladder, so I worked my way to the number one spot: Jack himself. In those days, there was literally a *jack* (my voice) in the *box* (the drive-thru ordering system). If an employee was esteemed enough to be *Jack*, then he had to alter his voice to a high-pitched shrill when he took customer orders. Whenever a car appeared in the drive-thru, I changed my voice to that of an eight-year-old girl, and said, "Hi, this is Jack! May I take your order?" Can you imagine this?! I was in tenth grade! This was possibly the worst job for my reputation at school, but I needed a job to help support my mom.

In 1967, I entered my first year of high school and it was an exciting time. Looking back, I realize that I enjoyed this year because it was filled with innocence. I went to high school dances called sock-hops and I also enrolled in Driver's Ed, Guidance and Health classes. It was a good year for me. I wanted a healthy lifestyle, so I tried to stay away from drugs. I wanted to get involved with sports as well; I was a good runner, so I thought I'd try out for the football team. I really wanted to play soccer, but chose not to because it was only played by recent immigrants and ESL (English Second Language) students. Plus, Roosevelt didn't have an organized team.

Wanting the all-American experience, I went out for the football team. I was inspired to check it out after someone saw me kick a football during P.E. and suggested that I try out for the Rough Riders' kicker position. I decided to go out for the team, but when I arrived at tryouts, I saw Jose Pelota. Now,

Jose was a big, ugly guy who played soccer with me in the City Terrace Soccer League and I couldn't stand him! We weren't rivals, but competing for the kicker position made me not like the guy. The tryout was straightforward enough: the person who kicked the furthest field-goal would become the team kicker. I tried with all my might, but Jose out-kicked me by one (ONE!) foot. There's a small part of me that's still a little bitter because in 1969, Roosevelt High went to the All-City Championship Game and played against San Fernando High. The game was played at East Los Angeles College and was one of the biggest classics back then. I can't help but think that I would have made the team if it wasn't for that one foot.

Ramblin' Gamblin' Man

"Yeah, I'm gonna tell my tale, come on,
Come on, yeah, well give a listen
'Cause I was born lonely down by the riverside
Men spin fortune wheels, and throw dice
I was only 13 when I had to leave home
Knew I couldn't stick around
I had to roam.
Ain't good looking, but you know I ain't shy..."

BOB SEGER

I wasn't able to play other sports because I had to work and because I had an unusually long commute to school. In order to get to Roosevelt, I had to catch two buses from South Los Angeles and it wasn't until my senior year—when I spent most of my days with my friend's family in Boyle Heights—that I had a somewhat reasonable commute. My

41

roommate worked at the first *McDonald's* in East Los Angeles (Lorena Avenue and Whittier Boulevard) and I worked at *Jack in the Box*, and often we competed to see who could steal the most money. Back then, stealing was easy because every transaction was done through a manual register, not the automated systems of today. I write about this thievery openly, but I am still embarrassed to admit it. Today, I speak with a clean conscience because after I gave my life to the Lord, I went back to my *Jack in the Box* and apologized to the manager for stealing money eight years prior. I told the manager—who didn't know me—that I was willing to pay back what I owed, but he just stared at me in complete disbelief. Trying to determine if I was drunk, joking or just plain crazy, he told me that paying back an eight-year-old debt was unnecessary. Since then, I can walk into a *Jack in the Box* without feeling guilty and enjoy my hamburger in peace.

Because I worked hard (and stole a little), I was able to dress sharply in high school. I never brought a lunch to school because I had money. But while I looked good on the outside, I didn't feel good on the inside. I resented the fact that I *needed* to work—which impeded my involvement with sports and school clubs—in order to support myself and help my mother with her expenses. I didn't have the luxury of going to sporting events, or putting on a sports uniform; I didn't have cheerleaders or family members rooting me on. I *had* to work. I resented parents who picked up their children from school and I resented not having a father to ask how I was doing academically. I resented other students' family-support structure because while they were earning straight A's, I was earning minimum wage and I had straight D's to show for it. Having no one to support me, financially or emotionally, brought forth another downfall.

In the summer of 1968, I became romantically involved with a girl on a serious level. She was a gorgeous girl and the best part was that she thought I was gorgeous too!

In hindsight, I realize we weren't in love; we were just two lost souls from broken families. Our days—and some nights—were spent with each other without a care in the world. We were left alone to act as husband and wife without legalities or boundaries. During this time, I began hanging out with the wrong group of people. This group followed me back to school in the fall of 1968, when the Vietnam War was in full swing.

Every morning Roosevelt High School's principal made the morning announcements over the public announcement system. After the familiar sound of the triple *ding, ding, ding* on the xylophone ended, the principal relayed the morning's news as well as how many former students died in the Vietnam conflict. Every day we had a moment of silence for alumni who died the previous day. However sad it was, when a soldier fresh from boot camp visited the campus, students flocked to him and I envied the praise he received. I wished for people to embrace me in the same way. It was the need to feel admired that kept the relationship with my girlfriend going. Although I was unfaithful and sexually active with other girls at the same time, she still stayed with me and I craved her dependence.

I don't remember too much from 1969 except a lot of partying—it was the year of Woodstock, after all. This was the year I let my hair grow long and, with my new look, I began a new job: selling drugs. I started selling *reds* and *yellow jackets* (barbiturates otherwise known as "downers") and used them myself regularly. I, however, never carried the drugs or cash myself. I had the *floozy* girls sell the drugs and the *school idiots* handle the money for me. Everyone in school knew I was dealing, but school officials couldn't prove it.

Later that year, my girlfriend dumped me. Some might dismiss this high school drama as unimportant, but I can't describe how much it hurt me. I was devastated. Although I was cheating on her, I couldn't believe she had the audacity to leave me. She was my first serious girlfriend and we planned on getting married. I can't remember how often we went to the reception hall/nightclub *Old Dixie* on Western and 42nd and convinced ourselves that we were meant for each other. We would *ooh* and *ahh* about getting married at St. Lucy in City Terrace and, yes, we planned to have a 6:30 p.m. reception at the Rodger Young Auditorium on Washington Boulevard. Everything seemed perfect until she dumped me.

The breakup caused me to go into a downward spiral and, consequently, fueled my recklessness; I slept with anyone. Drugs and alcohol were also permanent fixtures in my life.

When fall 1969 rolled around, I didn't know where I was headed and it frightened me. For the first time in my life, I was forced to make a hard, life-changing decision. I was 17 years old; I didn't have good grades and I was in trouble with the police. I was still doing drugs and I began urinating blood, an obvious indicator of alcohol abuse. All of a sudden, Vietnam didn't seem so bad. The Marines were an escape from life in East Los Angeles and, in September 1969, I enlisted in the 180-day delayed program at the ripe age of 17.

The Long and Winding Road

"The long and winding road that leads to your door
will never disappear.
I've seen that road before, it always leads me here."

THE BEATLES

In 1970, I graduated from Roosevelt High School. Typical of immigrant graduates back then, I couldn't read or write properly. Many of us shouldn't have graduated. But, in 1970, students were just pushed out of high school with passable grades and GPAs inflated by a heavy load of auto and metal shop, upholstery or wood shop or home economics. A faithful shop student, I had about three birdhouses, a large ceramic ashtray and the ability to rewire a car. Following graduation, I immediately joined the Marines Corps. This was the first significant alteration to my life. After graduating from Marine boot camp, I went home for my 30-day leave and received my Military Occupational Specialty (MOS) orders in the mail.

I was to become a Landing Vehicle Tank (LVT)

driver, an amphibian troop carrier. Once I completed LVT school, I was to be shipped to Vietnam. During the 1970s, the worst thing a Marine could read on his orders was *WESTPAC*, or Western Pacific. WESTPAC was another way of stating that Vietnam was the heading point of deployment. I was excited when I received my WESTPAC orders and was assigned to my platoon. A platoon would be together for four or five months and travel together to their destination. My platoon was scheduled to fly on American Airlines to Okinawa (an island off the coast of Japan) then to the Philippines and finally to Vietnam. However, something happened to my platoon in Okinawa. This was the hand of God. Upon our landing, we received new directives: half of the platoon was to remain in Okinawa and the rest were to resume with the scheduled itinerary, in military parlance, to Vietnam. As much as I wanted to go to Vietnam to fight for the United States, I was in the group that stayed behind. While I had visions of protecting my country, God had other plans for me.

In Okinawa, the Amtrac Battalion stationed at Camp Schwab needed a driver and I was one of the best. Amphibian Track Vehicles, or *Hogs*, were troop carriers that splashed down from the rear of a Navy ship and enabled vehicles to land on the beach shore. These vehicles would drop a ramp to let frenzied and combat-ready Marines run to the beach-landing zones. I was good at my job and was soon promoted to crew chief, which put me in charge of the commanding officers' vehicle.

It wasn't until eight months later that my platoon came together again at 10-7 Kadena Air Force Base in Okinawa. Although my platoon was made up of guys from different states—Michigan, Illinois and Nebraska—we became very close. When we met again at Kadena, I knew they were entirely different men than the pre-Vietnam boys six months earlier. They saw and did things in Vietnam few could ever understand. They had a look about them; a look that embodied firefights and gun-point deaths all before the age of 19.

Six months after arriving in Okinawa, it was my turn to leave for Vietnam. I was informed that my platoon was to be on the frontlines, but it didn't work out that way. My platoon joined a naval armada, a Battalion Landing Team (BLT), called Pacific Float, off the coast of Vietnam. This on-going operation continues to the present day, 24 hours a day, seven days a week, in seas around the globe.

This assignment initially seemed like a good thing for me, but it wasn't. True to sailor stereotypes, whenever the ship landed, I immediately sought women and booze, port after port. In these ports, I had access to any type of drug and sexual fantasy I wanted. I also went to Olongapo City, Philippines, a place referred to by Marines as the *Sodom and Gomorrah of the Pacific.* Perversity abounded at every corner and reared its wild head when I beckoned. I was alone. I was on the other side of the world and I missed home. I was only 18 years old and had the freedom to do whatever I wanted.

During the war, the American government supplied beer and, while I wasn't old enough to drink legally, I was permitted to indulge. The philosophy at the time was that if I was old enough to carry a rifle and put my life on the line, I was old enough to drink. My buddies and I would get drunk every night and then score drugs and illicit sex. These activities occurred around the world—Thailand, Japan, Singapore and the Philippines—and literally ruled my life.

In 1973, I was honorably discharged and I realized that I was no longer a boy, but a man. I left the Marines as a corporal, serving with honors. All my buddies thought that I was going to re-up because I was a *Marine's Marine,* a jarhead at heart. When I joined, I enlisted for three years, but I only did two years, nine months and 19 days. When I received my discharge, I went back to my unit, got my seabag and uniforms, and went back to the huts. At the huts, I said, "Hey! I ain't staying in the Marines—Bye suckers!!" I left the Marines that day, but the Marines have never left me.

Reelin' in the Years

"Your everlasting summer you can see it fading fast
So you grab a piece of something that you think is
gonna last.
You wouldn't know a diamond if you held it in your
hand
The things you think are precious I can't
understand..."

STEELY DAN

I returned to East Los Angeles from Vietnam in 1973 wanting to make up for lost time. From 1973 to 1975, all I did was party. This desire to party inspired me to enroll at East Los Angeles College (ELAC). Everyone knew that ELAC was a party school. Think of it as a high school with ashtrays. The nights when I didn't do homework, which was every night, I went out to clubs and partied hard. I was only 20 years old at the time, so in order to get into clubs like *Goldust,*

Kabuki's or *Monterey West,* I had to bribe the doormen. Like today's young people, my friends and I went to these clubs and acted foolishly. We paid to get into clubs, paid for expensive drinks and danced in dark rooms with strangers. Nothing's changed; it was and continues to be such a waste of money. I used to club every night and, for this reason, money was always tight before payday. Whenever I didn't have cash, I went to these clubs and spied on tables where a group of people were drinking. When the group got up from the table to dance, I slithered over to the table and stole their drinks. What a miserable life!

During my years at ELAC, drugs, alcohol and women were the lords of my life. I was making a lot of money selling drugs on the side, so this freed me up to do things that I loved doing. At the time, my passion was playing percussion, mainly the *congas* at Griffith Park every Sunday. My Sundays weren't filled with God, but, rather, with drugs, alcohol and women—idols I worshipped then.

In 1973, I saw the finest girl I had ever seen in my life. She had red hair down to her waist, hazel eyes and a beautiful smile. We vaguely knew each other by way of a mutual friend, but because so many guys hounded her I never had the nerve to speak to her. Her name was Mildred, or Millie, as her friends called her. She was a Los Angeles City College student majoring in theater arts, but I saw her at an ELAC dance. I watched her from the corner of my eye most of the night as she worked her way around the dance floor. Millie loved to dance, and jokingly attributed her moves to her Puerto Rican heritage. I was the type of guy who never danced, so I stood against the wall mesmerized. But, I wasn't the only guy that night struck by her beauty. Because of this, I stubbornly decided I would not to give her the satisfaction of pursuing her.

A few weeks later, we were both at a party and she saw me from across the room and instantly fell in love. Yeah right! I wish that was the case because, although I have a hard time admitting it, it was the other way around. That night, she came up to me and asked me why I never spoke to her and I replied: "Why should I?" Needless to say, it wasn't the impression I wanted to give. I thought that Millie was one of the most beautiful girls I had ever encountered and she, unlike other girls, didn't go out of her way to talk to me. She had this air about her that made me feel simultaneously wonderful and worthless. In spite of this, I still wanted to talk to her. I knew she was going to be at the party, so I ironed my most treasured cream-colored polyester pants, wore my favorite silk Hawaiian button-up shirt and donned my three-inch platform shoes. I made sure my hair was blown out (with my mother's hairdryer) the way Tony Orlando did his hair and I splashed on extra *English Leather* in hopes of being close enough for Millie to smell me. For a while, I thought that my dark hair and stylish clothes were what won her heart. But, I know now, that it was God's plan to get us together. Little did I realize that Millie wasn't just a beautiful girl, she would eventually be the woman who God would use to bring me to Christ.

Millie was one crazy chick back then—we drank, cursed and smoked too much weed together. She came from a good family and had a solid Catholic upbringing. But, in less than a year, we were sexually involved with each other. Our relationship was going well until one day, out of the blue, she told me that she was pregnant. Instead of being really angry or hurt, I was extraordinarily happy. I knew from the moment she told me that I wanted to take care of her and our baby, so I quit school and worked 19 hours a day.

I had one job as a playground director and another job working on an assembly line at an aluminum can company. I can't even begin to describe how much I hated working at the aluminum plant. I hated it! I hated the sights, sounds and atmosphere of the plant. But, none of this mattered when I thought of my baby on the way. I worked the night shift at the plant. Every night, after I punched my timecard, I stared at the clock on the discolored wall waiting for the hands to move. I worked these long hours to ensure that my child would be born at a decent hospital and not at Los Angeles County Hospital. It seemed that every child born out of wedlock in East Los Angeles was born at the County Hospital, so I did everything I could to not have my baby born there.

A couple of months later, Millie told me that she couldn't go through with the pregnancy. She worried for her family and her reputation, so she suggested an abortion. While I realized I was a hoodlum and a low-life, I also knew I had honor and dignity. I told

Millie she couldn't have an abortion, but she worried her family would abandon her. I told her that even if her family disowned her, she still had me and the baby in her life. I desperately tried to convince her to run away and marry me and I swore that I would take care of her and our baby. After much thought and many tears, she decided to go ahead with the abortion.

This situation scarred me and, once again, I was hurt by someone I loved. Instead of showing my pain, I built a wall with stones of anger and resentment. The day of her abortion I swore to myself that she— or anyone else for that matter—was never going to hurt me again. Millie made arrangements to go to the abortion clinic and, on that day, not one, but three people died.

After the procedure, a nurse wheeled Millie out to my Volkswagen and buckled her into the passenger seat. I gripped the steering wheel so tightly that my knuckles turned yellow, as I willed myself not to speak to her. As we rode in silence, Millie turned to me and asked if I could stop and buy feminine napkins for her. *Great, just great*, I thought to myself. *First she wants to stomp on my heart, now she wants to humiliate me!?* I was so embarrassed walking down the feminine products aisle; I felt as if everyone knew what had just happened and shook their heads with disapproval. As I stood in the pharmacy line, I swore to never see her again. When I dropped her off at home later that night, I told myself that was the last time I would ever see her. I didn't know then that the last thing Millie needed was someone to walk away from her.

What she needed was a friend; someone to hold her hand and support her. Crushed by what happened, my girlfriend searched for her best friend, but I was nowhere to be found.

Millie called my house and wrote letters to me, but I told her I wouldn't speak with a murderer. I was cold and cruel; self-hatred and fear fueled my actions. When Millie found me, she begged for forgiveness. I said I forgave her, but I told her I never wanted to see her again. She walked away from me that day and I didn't see her again until four months later.

Day By Day

"Day by day
Oh Dear Lord
Three things I pray
To see thee more clearly
Love thee more dearly
Follow thee more nearly
Day by day"

GODSPELL

During our time away from each other, Millie sought the company of a mutual friend who was a Christian. She invited Millie to church and led her to Christ. When I got word that Millie was going to church, I thought to myself, *She can go to church all she wants, but she's still going to Hell for what she did!* I was bitter, angry and disturbed with everyone and everything. I thought that Millie was someone who would never hurt me, but her actions shattered my security. I couldn't even think of her, so I pursued any woman who came my way. Millie's actions made my heart so hard, that I never wanted to feel love again.

When I saw Millie again, I immediately recognized a change. She was wearing a bra! I know this must sound terribly tacky, but it's the truth! Back in the 1970s, near the end of the Hippie movement, women wouldn't wear bras. So, when I saw Millie dressed modestly, with her hair nicely combed, and her dignified countenance, I knew she was different. When we met eye-to-eye, Millie told me that she fell in love with another man and to make things worse, he loved her unconditionally. She went on to share her love for Jesus Christ, who had transformed her life. Millie said she wasn't going to see me for six months. Although she still loved me, she had to let me go so that I would fall into the hands of God. She knew that if she were to hang out with me again, I'd talk her out of going to church and instead talk her into getting high. I tried convincing her that my weed and my wine were far better than church, but she faithfully ignored my pleas and chose to attend Bible studies instead.

After Millie's numerous rejections, I became angry and told her that she was brainwashed and I was tired of hearing about Jesus like He was her long-lost buddy. I was tired of hearing about God and the Bible. Around Christmas time, I asked Millie on a date and I bought her a special gift. On our date, we were at Griffith Park and the afternoon was unfolding nicely, until it was time to exchange gifts. I bought an expensive bottle of scotch for Millie and had it wrapped in a brightly colored box with a red bow. Millie slowly untied the ribbon and I became excited at the prospect of getting loaded. The gift that Millie brought for me was lying next to her and I secretly wished that she bought me scotch glasses. When Millie lifted the bottle, she softly touched the label and handed it back to me. She smiled and told me she had no use for such a gift, but appreciated the gesture. I was so infuriated that I wanted to throw the bottle. After a brief moment of uneasiness, she handed me my gift with gleeful anticipation. I unwrapped the gift only to find that Millie had bought me a Bible. A Bible?! I was so angry, I grabbed the Bible and threw it at her face. The Bible hit her face as her hazel eyes looked on tearful and hurt. I was enraged. I told her never to mention God, the Holy Spirit or her new boyfriend Jesus Christ to me ever again. I asked how she could murder our baby, hurt someone she loved, backstab a person and claim that God had forgiven her? It just seemed too easy. She tried telling me that God would forgive me too, but for six months, we went back and forth with each other.

Many times I called Millie at 3 a.m., on the verge of vomiting after a drinking binge, and asked her to join me. She told me again and again she would not join in my own self-destruction, but she would pray for me. Every time she told me this, I begged her to pray with me. Deep in my heart, I knew I needed prayer because I hated the world, Millie, and me. Millie would fall silent and then begin to pray. This happened so often that I became used to standing in various payphone booths around East Los Angeles in the wee hours of the morning. Often times, I was so drunk that I believed I could serenade Millie into falling in love with me again. *"If you loooose me, Oh yeah,"* I'd sing Barbara Lynn's song, *"You'd lose a good thing."* I begged her to stay with me the night, but she, as always, declined and the line would go dead. At this moment, I would stumble back to my Volkswagen, that reeked of *Brut* cologne and *Tommy's Burgers,* vomit and fall asleep in the backseat. This went on for months.

When I saw Millie again, I recognized greater changes and suddenly became painfully aware of my deterioration. She was growing and I was dying. I saw the contrast of light and darkness and it created an empty feeling in my heart. Whenever Millie tried leading me to Christ, I insisted that I couldn't understand how God could love someone like me after the wrong I'd done. I was ignorant and the only thing I understood was that I was dead to Christ. Millie told me about the depth and width of God's love, but I couldn't grasp it. Maybe it was stupidity or maybe it was that I didn't *want* to understand. In accepting God's love, I had to let go of the anger and resentment I had toward my mother, my father, my stepfather, Millie, and everyone else who wronged me. Millie brought out a Bible (the Bible that I threw in her face six months earlier) and read me *1 Corinthians 2:14, The man who isn't Christian cannot understand and cannot accept these thoughts from God which the Holy Spirit teaches. They sound foolish to him because only those who have the Holy Spirit within them can understand what the Holy Spirit means.* When Millie shared these words with me, I didn't have God in my heart, so nothing she said made sense. She told me that the minute I opened my heart to believe in God, He would open my eyes to better see Him and to better understand His word. It seemed so easy, but it was so hard!

Millie said she no longer needed religion to get to God because she had a *relationship* with Him. This made me angry and defensive, so I told her I already knew everything I needed to know about Jesus. Then, the worst thing happened: Millie asked me to tell her about Jesus. Dumbfounded, I told her that He was a Jew and a carpenter, his last name was Christ and that many movies had been made about Him. When I couldn't think of anything else to say, she told me I knew nothing of the God in which she believed. She told me I needed to believe *in* Him to have a relationship *with* Him. With all the machismo and bravado I could muster, I rolled my eyes and walked away.

I Can See Clearly Now

"I can see clearly now, the rain is gone,
I can see all obstacles in my way.
Gone are the dark clouds that had me blind.
It's gonna be a bright, sun shiny day.
I think I can make it now, the pain is gone.
All of the bad feelings have disappeared.
Here is the rainbow I've been prayin' for.
It's gonna be a bright, bright sun, shiny day…"

JOHNNY NASH

On May 6, 1975, Millie took me to a *rock concert*.
But the only *rock* present was the solid rock foundation
of Jesus Christ. I turned to Millie and called her a liar
when we pulled into the parking lot of Calvary Chapel
Costa Mesa. She had taken me to a church instead of
a concert. During the 1970s, Calvary Chapel Costa
Mesa was involved in the *Jesus Movement* and provided
a non-threatening and non-churchlike environment

for young people, including hippies, to make peace with God.

I wanted to leave as soon as we arrived, but Millie and I were joined by a group of her friends, so I was stuck. I felt stupid walking into church, but I felt even more stupid because I was: (1) still a little high from the joint I smoked before Millie picked me up; (2) a non-Christian; and (3) the only guy in the group. We sat in the sixth row of the sanctuary and when I looked around, I realized I couldn't make a quick exit. As Millie and her group of friends socialized, my only thought was the cigarette I was going to smoke in the church parking lot later that evening. I even planned what I would tell Millie if she asked me to not smoke in the church parking lot: "Holy smokes, Millie! It's just a holy lighting ceremony!"

During the service, Pastor Chuck Smith spoke about a man in the Bible named Daniel and the emptiness he experienced. Daniel was a man of God who prayed incessantly, without regard to the social constructs of the time, despite being persecuted for his beliefs. God's undying love allowed Daniel to remain steadfast in the faith. God delivered Daniel from the danger he was in and used Daniel's life as a testament to His great power. I had never heard the story of Daniel explained in such a way and I felt the strings that held my heart together being pulled apart. When the pastor gave the invitation to go forward and accept Jesus as my savior, my first reaction was to look away because I felt that he was staring straight at me. In my mind, no one in that huge sanctuary needed

God more than me. In addition, I seriously thought Millie had visited the pastor beforehand and told him to direct his sermon to me. Throughout the course of the service, I felt like the pastor kept one eye on me and the other eye on the rest of the congregation. When the pastor asked again if anyone wanted to form a relationship with Christ, I slowly inched my way out of my sixth row seat and walked forward. While a part of me felt like I was moving involuntarily, another part of me consciously realized I needed to give God a chance. I wanted to understand how the Holy Spirit could change my life.

I recited the sinner's prayer with a group of people and I felt good. There were no fireworks, I didn't fall down shaking; I simply felt good. But, I still questioned what I was doing. As I said the sinner's prayer, I attached my skepticism to the words. I prayed something like, "*If* you are God, then please forgive me; *if* you can wash me of my sins, then I ask you to do so; *if* there is a *Book of Life* and *if* I can be included, then please list my name." Afterward, I was guided into a small room and greeted by a new believer counselor. My counselor was a tall surfer with long blonde hair and he told me, "Oh, dude, your sins are like, forgiven. Everything is washed away, man! Like, whatever you did, dude, was in like the dark, but now you're in the light." To be honest, I didn't have the slightest clue what he was saying, but I felt good.

I woke up the next morning and craved my usual Sunday morning breakfast: a cold beer and a chorizo burrito. And, instead of experiencing spiritual enlightenment, my life went back to normal. In fact, I was worse off than before I accepted Christ because I was accountable for my actions having heard the Word of God. I still partied, smoked weed and got drunk a few days after accepting the Lord. But this changed about a week later when my life got flipped upside down on May 12, 1975. Instead of going to church that Sunday, I packed my *congas* in the back of the car and drove to Griffith Park to play with a group of musicians. It was a bright afternoon and all the regulars were there with their instruments and a stash of marijuana in their back pockets. We began to play and a joint was passed my way. I unabashedly took a hit and when I finished, I freaked out because something tasted funny, like aluminum. My first thought was that the joint was laced with something harder and I was scared that I would have a bad trip. But, after a few minutes, nothing happened. I looked around to see if the other guys were tripping out, but instead I noticed for the first time that these guys were messed up—even more than me! I looked around at the company I was keeping and realized they were druggies and alcoholics. For the first time in my life, I saw these people were bad news. Bothered by the bad taste of the weed and the realization that I was hanging out with total losers, I grabbed my *congas* and raced to my car. I was confused because after months of making music and smoking out with these guys, I never saw them for who they were: aimless men crippled by drugs and alcohol.

As I sat in the front seat of my car, I became more

upset because I didn't want to think I was better than my friends. I was so confused that the only thing I wanted to do was smoke a joint alone, in the solace of my car. I slipped my fingers underneath the driver's seat and pulled out what I called my *emergency joint*. When I lit and took a hit of the joint, it tasted so bitter that my tongue became numb. *What is going on here?!* I thought to myself. I didn't know this back then, but God was working in my life. Creeped out by my inability to smoke either joint, I threw the joint out the window and left Griffith Park in a hurry. I can't really explain what happened next because it was something supernatural. As I was driving over a bridge in Los Angeles, I rolled down my window and then reached into my glove compartment and grabbed the bag of marijuana I kept there. With my left arm stretched outside the window, I tilted the open Ziploc bag and watched green particles escape from their plastic prison and dance onto the black pavement.

72

I Don't Know How to Love Him

"I don't know how to love him.
What to do, how to move him.
I've been changed, yes really changed.
In these past few days, when I've seen myself, I seem
    like someone else.
I don't know how to take this."

MARY MAGDALENE, JESUS CHRIST SUPERSTAR

God started doing amazing things in my life. Yes, turning away from drugs was a battle and I still continued to struggle with smoking and drinking, but God gave me strength every day. Millie and I went to Calvary Chapel Costa Mesa every Sunday and we began to grow spiritually. I loved going to church to hear the Word of God brought to life. There were times in my young walk with Christ when I would come out of church and excitedly turn to Millie and say, "That was a d**n good sermon!" Millie, being

73

the wonderful girlfriend that she was, encouraged me in hushed tones to try to express my joy differently. Although we loved going to Calvary Chapel Costa Mesa, the 50-minute one-way commute from East Los Angeles began to take its toll. We decided that in order for us to become involved at church, it would be better for us to attend a Baptist church located closer to us. It was during this time that we became heavily involved with church and my relationship with Millie blossomed. I asked Millie for her hand in marriage and, much to my delight, she said yes.

God Given Love

"*I am for you*
You are for me
Together we stand oh, for all our lives
When I saw you,
When you saw me,
We both fell in love for all our lives.
I commit myself unto you.
You commit your love back to me."

MICHAEL GONZALES

On November 6, 1976, Millie and I married. We were in love and had no doubt that God wanted us together. We didn't have money for a traditional wedding, but we decided to make do with what we had. We didn't have money for a reception, so we filled our church's basement with folding chairs and tables and had a potluck dinner. A potluck dinner reception!!

And to make things worse, the church we attended did not allow dancing, so basically our reception consisted of eating everything, from rice and beans, to fried chicken and potato salad, while listening to worship songs sung by church members. Upon seeing the reception such as it was—and coupled with the fact that we didn't allow alcohol to be served—our non-Christian family members and friends thought we were in a cult. In retrospect, I understand why they thought we were weird. Nevertheless, God has used our marriage throughout the years to minister to those same people who laughed at our reception when their marriages began falling apart.

Married life was good. We had our ups-and-downs, but God sustained us. We bought our first home in Rowland Heights, California and we couldn't have been happier. I had a new joy knowing that I could cut *my* lawn, trim *my* trees, and sweep *my* porch. For the first time in my life, I owned something. Sure, I still had 356 payments left before I technically owned it, but at least it was *mine*! Everything was hunky-dory, Millie and I kissed before we left for work, kissed when we got back home, and kissed before I left for night school at East Los Angeles College where I majored in Hotel and Restaurant Management because I dreamed of owning my own restaurant. Not just any restaurant—I wanted to open a fine dining Mexican restaurant in Big Bear, California. I dreamed of the mouth-watering menu. I knew what the murals on the walls would look like. I envisioned knowing my customers' names by heart. Because Millie supported my dream and we seemed financially stable, we strived to reach this goal.

For Once in My Life

"For once in my life
I won't let sorrow hurt me
Not like its hurt me before, oh
For once I have something I know desert me
Cause I'm not alone anymore

For once I can say
This is mine, you can't take it
Long as I know I've got love I can make it
For once in my life
I've got that someone who needs me"

STEVIE WONDER

On a humid Saturday afternoon in 1979, I had just finished mowing the lawn when Millie came outside and put her arm around my sweaty shoulder. No sooner had we sat on the porch to admire my handiwork when she blurted out, "I'm pregnant!" I was excited to say the least.

But, while I was more than ready to be a father, I wasn't ready for the financial burden a child presented. Becoming a father altered my life yet again. On Easter Sunday 1980, Millie and I became parents to beautiful twin daughters, Jasmine and Bianca. When we first discovered that we were having twins, I remember being blown away by God's grace. Millie and I cried because in our ignorance we gave away one baby, but God—in His amazing grace—gave us two babies in return. I still think about the baby boy we decided not to have and how our family would have been different if he would have been a part of it. I know I'll see him again in Heaven and I draw comfort knowing that God's providence and control are magnificent, and this keeps me from feeling bitter. What we did in ignorance was forgiven. What an amazing lesson! Whatever sin a person commits, God can forgive. God gave us twins and we experienced what the prophet Joel spoke about in the Bible. In Joel 2:25, the Lord says "So I will restore to you the years that the swarming locust has eaten". What the cankerworm had eaten, the Lord gave back to us.

Happy Boy

"I have a car
It won't go very far.
But I don't care.
I can talk to Jesus anywhere.
Loving God makes me a happy boy.
I never need anything because loving God makes me a
*   happy boy.*
I never need anything because He takes care of me."

UNDERCOVER

Millie and I agreed that we wanted her to be a full-time mother, so she quit her job as a medical assistant. We tried to the best of our ability to properly scrimp and save, but when the babies were born, we were left searching for spare change between the couch cushions to make ends meet.

Creditors came to our door every week and, although I wanted to slam the door shut in their face,

God gave me the strength to maintain my composure. Still, we tried to make our monthly house payments by cutting back on groceries, hoping to postpone foreclosure. We cut back by making the most of an avocado tree in our backyard. Millie learned how to make avocado sandwiches, avocado soup, avocado quesadillas, avocado omelets—she might have even made avocado lasagna if she had found a recipe! Even with all our cutbacks and after much crying and begging the Lord to provide for us, we lost our house in 1984. With heavy hearts, we packed our bags and said goodbye to our American dream.

We moved into a small two-bedroom apartment in Baldwin Park, California. Millie was pregnant with our third child and the move was difficult for her. She was used to having a yard for the girls to play in, but the only grass the apartments offered was between the cracks in the sidewalk.

Millie missed the view from the front windows of the home we lost even more after realizing that a concrete wall was the only thing she could see from the apartment windows. The location wasn't the best and my daughter Jasmine made an interesting observation one Sunday morning driving home from our new church, Calvary Chapel West Covina. We lived on Badillo Avenue, so she turned to me and said, "Daddy, if you notice, the first three letters of our street name are B-A-D. This is probably because we live in a bad neighborhood." I let the truth of her statement sink in. This may seem like a lot for a five-year-old to discern, but she was quite bright.

Late one evening that holiday season, as my family and I drove home from the laundromat, we pulled into our carport and I sensed something wasn't right. When I reached the front door, I stood—frozen—as I realized that we had been robbed. Not just robbed, cleaned out!

There was <u>nothing</u> left. The thieves took everything, from the baby crib, to the stereo, to the bed linens, to Millie's wedding ring. As I took inventory of what was stolen, I desperately looked for some valuable lesson God wanted us to learn. Then it hit me: *Yes, Lord, I can and will still make Christmas dinner for my family. Christmas is about Jesus' birth, not material things.* I walked into the kitchen to find out whether the thieves had taken our pots and pans as well. Then, I heard the humming noise a refrigerator makes when the door has been left open. As I grabbed the handle to the freezer I thought, *No, no, they wouldn't...they wouldn't dare take...* And then, I yelled, "Millie! They stole our frozen turkey, too!"

I called the landlord that evening to change the locks on our door. I felt powerless, frustrated and desperate. I asked God what more He wanted of me. It seemed like He was taking everything I had—literally. That night, Millie found old blankets, laid them on the floor, and the girls fell asleep next to her as she rocked our new baby daughter, Alexandria Lavender, in her arms. Neither she nor I could sleep that night. I paced our 15-foot living room listening for betraying sights or sounds, while she prayed silently. The next morning, Millie and I prayed that God would deliver us from this apartment as soon as possible. He kept us there for another year before opening the door to a new home.

After the robbery, we searched desperately for a new home, but we couldn't even afford a matchbox. A friend at church told Millie about a home for sale in La Puente, California. So, just to pacify her, I promised we'd go take a look. A few days later, we visited the house and, although we loved it, we couldn't afford it. The house had been on the market for quite some time and the owner couldn't sell it for the asking price. When Millie and I left the house, she told me she believed the house was ours. I tried telling her gently not to get her hopes high, but she told me God was going to bless us. I didn't want to hurt her feelings, so I dropped the subject.

A few days later, we received a call from the owner. A dream, he said, revealed to him that we should move into the house. This might sound like a made-up story, but it's true. Just as God worked with Joseph in the *Old Testament* through dreams, God used a dream to show the owner that we were destined to live in this house. Millie practically bounced off the walls when I told her the good news. Jokingly, I asked her— since God was showing her many things—to inquire whether God was going to bless me with a Porsche. If God was speaking to Millie, why not ask about my dream car?! I didn't get the Porsche, but God still blessed our socks off. The Lord blessed us when the owner leased the house to us with the option to buy. In 1986, we moved into our new home and thanked God again and again.

Serve Somebody

"You may be an ambassador to England or France
You may like to gamble, you may like to dance.
You may be the heavyweight champion of the world
You may be a socialite with a long string of pearls
But you're gonna have to serve somebody.
Well, it may be the devil or it may be the Lord
But you're gonna have to serve somebody."

BOB DYLAN

Living in La Puente was a gift from God, but when much is given, much is required. Paying the mortgage when my wallet was nearly empty strained our finances, but God never let us down. Financial difficulties followed my family like a shadow. We lived paycheck to paycheck, but God never left our side. In fact, He picked us up when we thought we could no longer walk. I can't possibly recount how often members of our church would anonymously drop groceries on our front porch or leave a blank envelope with cash inside in our mailbox. Many a Christmas we found wrapped gifts on our porch addressed to our children and marked *From: Baby Jesus.* The Body of Christ at Calvary Chapel West Covina took care of my family; the church was the glue that kept our faith intact.

Even some of our neighbors recognized our financial struggle. One neighbor in particular blessed us continually. She was an older woman with a kind, round face and salt and pepper hair. Her name was Valentina and she lived with her husband across the street, a few houses over. Every so often, Valentina slowly walked down our block to give Millie a large container of lemon yogurt and a bag of oranges. Valentina never said much, but her kindness spoke volumes to my wife and children. Between her weekly donations, government-issued peanut butter and discounted bread, my kids always had lunch.

During this time, I was the leader for the Mexico outreach ministry at our church. Every two weeks, I led members of the church to orphanages and *colonias*— small towns—in the most decaying parts of Tijuana and Rosarito. We built homes and shared the gospel. This ministry sprouted from my love for Mexico and my deep desire to share God's Word. Millie was a true die-hard and helped me every step of the way. Before the ministry at church became official, she collected used clothes, blankets and toys from church members for our monthly trips to Baja. At the time, it was strictly a family trip, so we packed my Volkswagen van to the top with goods, making sure the kids weren't buried underneath, and headed south in the pre-sun hours of a bright Saturday.

Our goal was to visit a new *colonia* per visit, so we planned to get lost in the hills of Tijuana or Rosarito. While at first we didn't know how to distribute our goods, we soon figured out the best way to be charitable and share our love of God was through children. Driving through a *colonia*, we would spot a child walking and ask if he or she would like a toy. At first reluctant, the child would take the toy and immediately run home. Within minutes, our van would be swarmed by children prying their little fingers into our windows asking for toys from America. We encouraged our daughters to pass the toys out and tell the children—in Spanish—that Jesus loved them. There are no words to describe how proud I was to hear my children proclaim the love of God to other children.

To this day, my children thank me for exposing them to life in a third world country. They tell me the trips made them extraordinarily appreciative for their lives in the United States. No matter how tough times were for them—not playing sports or taking dance lessons, wearing hand-me-downs or shopping at a thrift store—they realized they were blessed.

The trips to Mexico with my wife and children propelled me into starting the Mexico ministry at church. I enjoyed serving in this ministry, but at the same time I wondered if it was the right thing to do.

I often accepted weekend jobs to supplement my meager income and because I was leading a church group to Mexico every other weekend, I was giving up much needed money. Just when I was questioning leaving the ministry to take on a steady weekend job, God performed a miracle in my garage.

During this time, my family was so strapped for money that we could barely afford groceries. Millie served potpies every other night for dinner because each frozen pie cost only $0.25, so on those evenings, the entire family ate for less than $2! I was convinced that I needed a steady weekend job to make ends-meet—and to get away from those potpies. But, just as I was about to leave the Mexico ministry, I received a phone call from Frank, a fellow Mexico ministry-worker. He referred me to the manager of a local grocery store who offered us food donations for our trips. I whole-heartedly agreed, but when he told me that I needed a permanent place to store the weekly food donations, I didn't know what to do. The grocery store gave us so many boxes of food that the church didn't have enough storage room for them and the ministry couldn't afford a storage facility. I didn't know where to turn. Then something amazing happened: the manager asked if I would be able to store the food in my garage. I wasn't sure if I heard right. *Food? In my garage!?* Then, as if this wasn't enough, he sweetened the deal by giving me whatever food I needed, as often as I needed. A couple of days later, my entire garage was brimming with boxes and boxes of groceries. Because of this miracle, I didn't have to buy toilet paper, guava juice, bread, guava juice, toothpaste, guava juice, fruit snacks, guava juice, or any canned food for more than a year! Did I mention guava juice? Before this backyard miracle, my family never drank guava juice, but when we got liter after liter, it became a refrigerator staple. After their 2,579[th] glass of juice, my kids would have preferred gulping down tar instead of the sweet pink liquid. Now that they are grown, I threaten them jokingly by saying, "Hey, you better calm down or I'll make you drink some guava juice!"

During this time, I worked for Los Angeles County in the shipping and receiving department at Los Angeles County/University of Southern California General Hospital. I worked 16 years for the hospital and had pretty much everything I needed—medical, vision and dental insurances, 401(k) retirement plan and vacation time. It was an easy job and I enjoyed the perks, but when the opportunity arose for me to make more money, I jumped at the chance. I left the county hospital to become a grief counselor at a funeral home in Glendora, California.

The funeral home director informed me he wanted a bilingual pastor to comfort the family members of the deceased, but I quickly discovered this was so far from the truth. What he really wanted was for me to sell coffins, flower arrangements and plots, not comfort families. I quit the same day. I couldn't believe that a funeral home would disguise a sales job as a pastoral position and I was struck numb with the horrible career choice I had made. I went back to the county hospital and asked for my job. But 16 years of hard work made no difference. I couldn't get my job back; the county was experiencing a hiring freeze.

For the first time in my life, I was without a job. I began working as a paperboy when I was 10 years old, so this was a new and lonely crossroad in my life. After leaving the county hospital and quitting my job at the funeral home, I had no where to go. I had no money and no job prospects. After walking out of the funeral home on that hot summer day, I pulled off the freeway and called Millie from a telephone booth. I was sobbing so desperately that she couldn't understand a single word I said. After catching my breath, I tried telling her what had happened and I confessed that I didn't know what to do. As a father, a man, and as the sole provider for the Juarez family, I had failed miserably. Millie prayed for me and asked God to show us what to do. Her strength humbled me because she was home-schooling our three daughters and was eight months pregnant with our fourth child. She didn't know what trials lay ahead, but she confidently approached God in faith and asked Him to lead the way.

I searched for jobs with health insurance coverage knowing that in a month my wife would need a C-section to deliver our child. Few companies offered health insurance and, if they did, it took 90 days for the policy to kick in. Millie didn't have 90 days to spare. I looked high and low for a job with health insurance coverage and finally I found a position at Azusa Pacific University. The job—cafeteria cook—was a blessing on many levels, but most importantly because the health insurance was effective immediately. But, the job only paid $7.20 an hour. *Seven* dollars an hour to support three children and a wife with a baby on the way! But God never let us down.

There were some days when I drove to work and dreaded the idea of making oatmeal and scrambled eggs for privileged college students who referred to me as Paco, Jose or *señorito*. One day I was so overwhelmed with financial stress and anxiety that I stumbled into the walk-in freezer and cried while standing in front of frozen pieces of meat. I asked God "why?" *Why, Lord, must I always struggle? Why does it seem like the more I give to You, the more I strain?* I can't explain what happened that day, but I felt the peace of God like I never had before. I walked out of the freezer with bluish lips, and with a renewed sense of security because I knew God was going to take care of me. The Lord was on my side and I realized that though my life was difficult, I was still blessed. I was blessed with a home, a healthy family, a car (yes, it only worked on some days, but it was still a car!) and a stable job at a Christian institution. The best news was that my son, Sebastian Joel, was born healthy on January 16, 1992.

Most people wonder how my family sustained itself on such a meager paycheck. But, it was during this time that we truly saw God's hand moving mightily in our lives. As with many cafeterias around the United States, Azusa Pacific University's cafeteria threw away food on a daily basis. The cafeteria staff prepared lunch for almost 1,200 students and often overestimated. When I saw all the discarded food, I asked if I could take home the left-overs. With permission, I washed out empty cottage cheese containers and packed up our evening meals. When I pulled into the driveway every night, I was greeted by my three daughters eagerly anticipating that evening's dinner. They cheered when I brought home pizza, macaroni and cheese and pasta because prior to working at APU, I never had the money to buy such foods. The food I was allowed to take home became modern day manna for my family. We saw God miraculously put food on our table every night when we couldn't afford it. Times were tough for us, but God saw us through every situation.

It was during my time at Azusa Pacific University that I started teaching a home bible study in Montebello, California. The study grew over two years and in July 1992, I decided to have Sunday morning services. When I realized that the congregation was quickly growing, I asked my senior pastor from Calvary Chapel West Covina, Raul Ries, to send a pastor from his church to take over the fellowship. As we sat on the church pews in the back of the sanctuary, Pastor Raul looked at me as if I was crazy. He told me that I was the pastor of the church, but I just stared at him blankly. I tried telling him that I couldn't be the pastor because I thought God wanted me to have my own restaurant; God wanted me to drive a Porsche sports car; and live in Big Bear. He didn't want me to pastor a church in East Los Angeles! But, Pastor Raul insisted that God called me to the ministry, so instead of fighting it, I told God that I was ready for whatever He wanted of me.

The Battle Belongs to the Lord

"When the battle of darkness comes like a flood,
The battle belongs to the Lord.
When your enemy reaches land, do not fear
The battle belongs to the Lord"

JAIME OWENS-COLLINS

In 1994, just as the ministry began to flourish, the Lord surprised me with another blessing: at 42, I was going to become the father to another baby girl. At first, this news shocked Millie and me because we took proper precaution to avoid another pregnancy, but God had another plan. Once the initial shock passed, we were elated at the idea of adding to our family. Millie was 40 years old when she was pregnant with our daughter. Doctors worried that her age could compromise the baby's health. Shortly into the pregnancy, we got news that the baby wasn't developing normally. Millie's doctors wanted her to have an amniocentesis (extraction of amniotic fluid from a pregnant woman to aid in the diagnosis of fetal abnormalities) to find out what was wrong. When we told them that we were afraid of the test's potential effects on the baby, they told us that the baby might have *spina bifida* (a congenital defect in which the spinal column is imperfectly closed so that part of the spinal cord protrudes) and would likely be born mentally retarded.

The news of having a handicapped child shocked us. The sting of this realization made us beg and plead with God, but we never lost faith. The doctors encouraged Millie to terminate the pregnancy and when we declined, they asked us to abort the baby for its quality of life. The doctors insisted that this was the best decision for everyone involved, but they had no idea that the mere mention of an abortion carried years of pain and torment for us. An abortion was out of the question. I told the doctors that if God wanted to bless us with a mentally and physically disabled daughter, it was because He thought that we would be the best parents for her.

For seven painful months, Millie and I waited and prayed. There were dark days when Millie blamed herself for the pregnancy, especially bearing a child at her age. I reminded my wife that this baby was a gift and a promise from God. She was the embodiment of a covenant between me and the Lord. In the *Old Testament*, Abraham bore Isaac at a late age and God was merciful by adding years to his life. I told Millie that through our daughter the Lord was showing us that we were meant to remain on Earth for a while to work for the glory of His Kingdom.

Just before the birth of the baby, Millie had chosen a name for our daughter. Like our other daughters, she wanted to name the baby after a flower. Many years before, we agreed Millie would choose the names for our daughters and I would choose the names for our sons. But for this baby, I came across a name that I fell in love with: Zoe Belle. Regardless of whether our daughter would lead a normal life, this name suited her beautifully.

By God's grace and mercy, a perfect and healthy baby girl—without congenital abnormalities—was born on June 13, 1994. The doctors referred to this miracle as an "instantaneous resolution," but I corrected them—it was a miracle, plain and simple.

In the labor recovery room, Millie asked about the baby. I told her that our daughter was perfect, a miracle from God and a testament to our prayer and faith. Crying, Millie said, "Pancho, please let me see my little Lily Rose." I held the baby in my arms and said, "Well, there's no Lily Rose here, but there's a Zoe Belle." Millie looked at me suspiciously, as I went on to explain that in the Greek language, *zoe* means God breathed life, or a life God breathed upon. Millie took our daughter in her arms and knew that her name was perfect.

Sometimes

"Sometimes God answers Yes when we pray
Sometimes God answers Wait when we pray
Sometimes God answers No, just because he loves us so
Sometimes God answers Yes when we pray"

HYMN

After Zoe's birth, I quit my job at Azusa Pacific University to become a full-time pastor. The good news was that I was a pastor, but the bad news was that I didn't get paid for several months. During this time, we depended on God for everything—*everything*!

Millie and our children made a prayer chart with paint and brightly colored parchment paper. On this chart, our children catalogued every petition, every request and every thanksgiving to God. Every child listed a desire or concern and as the Lord answered them, they crossed out entries. It seemed silly at the time, but my children taught me a valuable lesson:

God <u>always</u> answers prayer. Sometimes He answers *yes*, sometimes He answers *no*, but He <u>always</u> answers prayer!

In their prayers, my children asked for everything from Christmas gifts, to the salvation of their grandparents, to a family car. The car request was something we all wanted because we drove a beat-up 1974 Volkswagen van that was given to us by a friend. My children didn't just want any car; they dreamed of being passengers in the back seats of a Toyota Previa family van. They knew the color they wanted (maroon), the year they wanted (1991) and even the breed of dog to accompany the van, just like the one they saw on the billboard we passed every day on the freeway. When we drove by this billboard, the kids *always* said that was the car God was going to give us. I sometimes had to swallow a laugh because there was no way we could ever afford such a car; then again, with God anything is possible. He taught me a HUGE lesson when I randomly received a phone call from a member of our church who worked in an auto repossession center. He called to say that he heard I was looking for a car and his company just received a van: a Toyota Previa family van, maroon in color, year 1991 and it even came with a dog! No, I'm just kidding about the dog, but everything else was a perfect fit. I placed a bid for the car and I won the silent auction by a mere $50. When my children returned to our *prayer chart* and scratched off their request for a family car, I was again reminded that God <u>always</u> answers prayer.

Saint Behind the Glass

"Hammer and a nail
Saint behind the glass
Holds a hammer and a nail

Baby in his arms
Baby in his arms
Saint behind the glass
Has a baby in his arms
Watches me sleep
Watches me sleep
Saint behind the glass
Watches me while I sleep"

LOS LOBOS

The lesson about prayer that I learned from my children was important because prayer was, and still is, the cornerstone of Calvary Chapel Montebello. After our home fellowship exceeded capacity, the church started to meet on Wednesday nights at a Montebello city park called Taylor Ranch. Yes, we literally congregated in a ranch and the children's ministry—ages five through 12—was housed in a barn divided into sections by the use of office cubicle dividers. The junior high class was held outside in a gazebo and, when the winter months approached, a blue tarp was hung from the inside to keep out the rain and the cold. The kids called it the *blue marble* and, while I was fond of the name, my heart sank when I heard the junior high students singing worship songs in the cold.

Taylor Ranch was primarily used by Montebello's senior citizens as an art house of sorts. The elderly painted pictures and hung them on the mustard-colored walls. Every week I was reminded by the artists not to touch the paintings or move them from their spots. This was a challenge because the place was so dirty it was nearly impossible to clean without moving things around. The floors were never mopped and the ranch had a nauseating smell of used lard and roach spray throughout.

On weekends, Taylor Ranch was rented out for parties and weddings and most of the time it wasn't cleaned properly after each use. The bathrooms smelled worse than the kitchen, and there were only two stalls—one for men and one for women. After meeting at Taylor Ranch a few weeks, I realized that the bathroom hallway never smelled clean, no matter how vigorously the clean-up crew scrubbed the toilets—when I mention the 'clean-up crew', I should probably note that this crew was comprised of my twin daughters and a single mom who consistently showed up early to clean and set up folding chairs. The good news is that the bathroom stench was finally addressed when I realized that attendees of Taylor Ranch's weekend parties would urinate in the hallway instead of waiting to use one of the two bathroom stalls. Once I figured this out, the clean-up crew's responsibilities extended beyond the bathroom stalls and into the hallway!

In the summer, the Ranch became unbearably hot. So hot, in fact, that members of our small congregation brought fans from home. And if this wasn't humbling enough, some brought reclining lawn chairs and sat outside the building under the windows in hopes of feeling the Santa Ana winds roll in.

One evening, an elderly gentleman stood up from his chair during the middle of service. He remained standing and I looked at him quizzically, hoping to elicit some sort of gestured response. He looked straight at me and said aloud, "I'm just too hot sitting down; I want to stand right here under this ceiling fan." Not wanting to make a scene, I went right along with the service. At the end of the sermon, I asked those who wanted to dedicate their lives to Christ to raise a hand. The standing gentleman raised his long arm and then—BAM—the ceiling fan whipped across his fingers. Needless to say, things did not go well that night.

Being a new pastor had its struggles, but I know that it also had an effect on my children. They were forced to live in a glass house and I thank them for following God despite the difficulties they faced while growing up. Trying to navigate the pre-teen labyrinth is hard enough on its own, but when one of my daughters struggled with weight-issues and was picked on by the boys in her youth group, I battled the urge to buy her boxing gloves. Instead, I told her that God loves us despite how mean we can sometimes be towards others and that she should try to turn the other cheek.

Late one Wednesday night, she ran out of cheeks to turn and made a terrible decision. The boys were playing a game in which they sprinted—full force— towards her, slamming against her with their body weight. After four boys followed in suit, the runt of the pack wanted to join in the game. My daughter had another thing in mind. As he ran toward her, she leaned back, absorbed his momentum and then lifted him away from her, sending him sailing through the air. The boy landed on his collar bone and was rushed to the emergency room. In all the commotion, nobody got the story straight. That is, of course, until I received a phone call around midnight from the boy's grandparents. All he could say in the emergency room was that my daughter broke his collar bone.

This was embarrassing because some of the people in church casually joked that my children were going to scare away the other children from Sunday school. They said this jokingly, but I realized that there was some truth to it.

My son, Sebastian, was known in the nursery as

a terror. When the toddlers and babies recognized him, they cried. Sebastian was infamous for biting other children and some mothers had taken the opportunity to rebuke Millie for not sitting in the nursery and watching our son. His canine teeth grew in first instead of his two front teeth. This caused his bite to appear as if it had been inflicted by Dracula instead of by a human toddler!

Other than breaking collar bones and biting babies, my children have grown up in the ways of the Lord. Thankfully, what my children did in ignorance was forgiven and they are humbled by the memories.

In the Holy Place

"In the holy place where we can enter in
By the blood of the Lamb
He has given us atonement for our sins
As a love gift sacrifice

Now let's sing
To the one who's called I Am
As we praise the Holy Lamb
As we lift our hands
In the Holy Place"

As quickly as my children grew, so did the congregation. We soon outgrew Taylor Ranch and began holding services on Sundays at Schurr High School in Montebello, California. We met in the auditorium and Sunday School was conducted in the school's classrooms. This was a wonderful move for the church.

I began to see how God worked in so many

different lives, all for His glory. There was such a diverse mix of people—former gang bangers, business owners, teachers, law enforcement—and everyone worked together in setting up and sustaining our church. There are still members of our church who remember our days at Schurr and together we look back and thank God for how far He has brought our ministry.

At the time, I thought my ministry was done growing. I thought that God wanted me to lead a small congregation and work on a small scale. But, when the auditorium was filled on two Sunday morning services and an evening service, I knew that God wanted us to find a building of our own.

I wondered if God really wanted me in Montebello, part of me continued thinking God would lead me to Big Bear to open my dream restaurant. For so long, I thought that the minute I had the opportunity to leave East Los Angeles, I would dart for the nearest exit. But, God had different plans for me. He took me on a boomerang path back to my old stomping grounds.

Starting a church was something I never intended. All I wanted was to start a Friday night home Bible study. It never crossed my mind that God would use me to share His gospel. Surely He could have found a man who was more skilled, educated and put together. I continued to pray that God would point me in the right direction because I felt so inadequate.

God quickly answered my prayers. All doubt vanished when He placed an empty trucking warehouse in my lap. Tucked in the southern-most-tip of Montebello, the building was owned by a Christian man who had been trying to sell it for some time. When I saw the large, gray building, I didn't want to get my hopes up because I had been turned away by other property owners who didn't want to sell their building to a church. Another doubt that crept into my mind was that the building was out of the church's budget. Located in the margins of East Los Angeles, and in an industrial area, it was prime business property.

As I walked through the building with my associate pastor, I prayed as I entered every room. I asked the Lord to please go before any transaction, wanting everything to be according to His will. At the end of the walk-through, the owner, the associate pastor and I prayed before we left. What a great way to end the meeting! The Lord heard us and opened the doors a few weeks later for Calvary Chapel Montebello. We purchased the building with practically no money. It was a true miracle. The building was a gift from God and it's where the congregation meets for services. I firmly believe that the only reason God gave the church this building was because we remained on our knees—in prayer—every step of the way.

It Is Well With My Soul

"When peace like a river attendeth my way
When sorrows like sea billows roll
Whatever my lot, Thou hast taught me to say
It is well, it is well with my soul

It is well
With my soul
It is well, it is well with my soul"

HORATIO G. SPAFFORD

The road a Christian walks is a series of mountains and valleys—extreme highs and desperate lows—often littered with painful potholes. In 1999, my family descended into a desolate valley and our lives changed drastically as we tried to navigate through desert lands.

Millie, otherwise in good health, began complaining of pain behind her eyes. Quickly dismissing these symptoms as allergies, she later became worried when she began suffering from inflamed ears and eyes. Millie's pain became more intense and her doctor suggested sinus surgery. But, after this operation, Mille got worse. We visited numerous doctors and they all told us something different—it seemed like she was diagnosed with everything from multiple sclerosis (a chronic degenerative disease of the central nervous system that occurs in patches throughout the brain or spinal cord, interfering with the nerve pathways, causing muscular weakness and speech and visual disturbances) to Graves disease (a condition usually caused by excessive production of thyroid hormone and characterized by an enlarged thyroid gland, protrusion of the eyeballs, a rapid heartbeat, and nervous excitability).

By 2000, Millie looked like someone held her under water too long. Her eyes bulged from her head, giving her the appearance of a goldfish, and her ears were so inflamed that they looked like large pieces of red cauliflower. Finally, a doctor at St. Jude Hospital in Fullerton, California, began to seek answers below the surface. He suspected that Millie had a growth behind her eyes that was affecting the normal functions of her face.

I was scheduled to lead a group from our church to Egypt and Israel when doctors decided to operate. As I planned to cancel the trip, Millie held my hand and encouraged me to go with the group. She said that God called us to the ministry and she wasn't going to allow Satan to disrupt what the Lord had started.

I was amazed—and still am—at Millie's faith, strength and resolve. As the doctors prepared Millie for the operation, she laid on the rolling hospital bed with fluorescent lights casting awkward shadows on her face. We held each other's hands and prayed that God would be merciful in His dealings with her. We knew that the surgeons were going to break part of her face to retrieve a biopsy of the growth; this would determine whether it was cancerous. We prayed for a quick healing and negative biopsy results. I prayed continuously while Millie underwent the procedure and when she was finally out, I left immediately to the airport. My flight to Egypt departed later that morning.

When I arrived in Cairo, Egypt, I called Millie and learned that cancer had formed behind her eyes. The news hit both of us like a ton of bricks. I desperately wanted to be with Millie, to hold her and assure her that everything was going to be fine. Instead, it was Millie who was offering the words of encouragement. She was scared, but she knew that God would use this experience for His glory and she trusted Him.

When I returned from Israel about a week later, Millie immediately started her cancer treatments with radiation. It was a slow process, but it wasn't as bad as we anticipated. Millie had to wear patches on her eyes and at home we jokingly called her *captain* or *pirate*. Through prayer and the undying support of our congregation, God guided Millie toward recovery. It wasn't until her radiation treatments were complete that we noticed things still weren't normal.

Instead of regaining balance and strength, Millie lost almost total control of her body. Her words were slurred and sounded as if her tongue was constantly in the way of her teeth. I tried to convince myself that things were normal—that this was just a bump on the road to remission—but one afternoon when Millie was asked to speak to a group at church, things became visibly worse.

Millie asked me to escort her on stage because she felt her legs would give out if she climbed the six steps leading to the stage. As she fraily held the microphone, I noticed that one side of her mouth appeared frozen, the way her mouth looked when she returned from the dentist after getting a cavity filled. She tried speaking normally, but drool began dripping down the side of her face. Millie stopped mid-sentence and desperately looked to me for help. For a split second, I didn't know what to do. Should I shield her from this embarrassment, should I hug her, should I pretend that nothing happened? I took over the presentation and wanted to keep talking forever because I knew that as soon as I stopped, I would have to face Millie's sickness head-on.

Millie and I visited what seemed like every specialist in California to determine what was wrong. Doctors referred to Millie as a medical puzzle and we were beginning to believe we wouldn't find a cure. Then a member of our church recommended that we visit a doctor at University of Southern California Norris Cancer Center in Los Angeles. Temporarily gripped by fear and skepticism, but grounded by faith and hope, we visited a doctor who is a modern day medicine man and miracle worker. Millie was at her worst when she visited Dr. Marc Chamberlain. And, with one look, he diagnosed her with lymphoma meningitis (cancer of the central nervous system). When we told Dr. Chamberlain that Millie underwent countless spinal taps, CT scans and MRIs without detecting cancer in her brain, he told us this type of cancer was rare and attacked a portion of the brain that is almost undetectable by way of standard testing. Even though Dr. Chamberlain admitted that the diagnosis was inconclusive, we decided to proceed with his recommended treatments.

Millie and I prayed over and over about her cancer treatment. She had to undergo brain surgery to have a shunt inserted in her skull for the chemotherapy to be administered. With God by her side, Millie left the operating room without hair, but with a brand new shunt peeking from underneath her scalp. While the original shunt was used for the administration of chemotherapy, in a later operation, Millie had a tube placed near the shunt (that stretched from her cranium, behind her ear, into her stomach), for the regulation of brain fluid.

The following two years were a series of ups and downs. Millie was undergoing two types of chemotherapy, one for the cancer in her brain and one for the cancer that persisted behind her eyes. This left her almost immobile and completely dependant on me and our five children. Everyone in my family dealt with this grief differently and I asked the Lord

Almighty for renewed strength daily.

My twin daughters were away at college, but they came home every weekend and sometimes during the week to help make meals and clean the house. My daughter Alexandria was in high school and dealt with her pain through isolation and detachment. The family tried to protect Sebastian and Zoe from the fact that Millie could die, but they knew that their mother—who once tucked them into bed every night—was dealing with something so aggressive she couldn't even get out of bed.

Sometimes I found my children crying in the darkness of their rooms fearing their mother dying. It was hard to blame them for feeling alone because seeing their mother incapacitated, without a concrete diagnosis, raised doubts and fears in all our minds. There were times when I would drive to church and cry in the car. Sitting in freeway traffic, I would beg God to heal my wife. I was tired of seeing Millie suffer and I asked God to take this thorn from her side. It was then when I realized that I was not to ask God for *substitution* (the replacement of something with something else), but, rather, God wanted me to ask for *transformation* (a complete change). God wanted to *transform* my mind and heart to better understand His ways. The Lord placed my family in the fire to refine, define, and keep us supine for the glory of His kingdom. Millie was like a caterpillar waiting to shed her barbed skin for butterfly wings. But change was slow and seeing her in this condition was painful. She faced one challenge after another as she fought to recover.

On one occasion, I was asked to speak at a church in San Diego and I thought it would be nice to get Millie out of the house. That day, she rose early, but as she got out of bed and tried walking to the bathroom, she fell. I was jolted out of my sleep when I heard the sounds of Millie falling against the hallway closet and, ultimately, to the floor. I rushed to her side and instead of saying that she was okay, she first apologized for making noise and waking me.

Her fall wasn't the first time something like that had happened. One afternoon, Millie slipped from the passenger seat into the gutter as she tried getting out of our car. Other times her legs turned to jelly while out in public and she clung onto anybody, or anything, that was around. Often times, I had to literally hoist Millie by her armpits when the nerves in her legs didn't work and pray that her strength would return swiftly. The struggle continued and her body deteriorated to the point where she couldn't even control her bowel movements. One painful afternoon, Millie, to her horror, couldn't control herself and defecated while in bed. As I cleaned her and changed the sheets, she looked at me apologetically and asked, "Pancho, do you love me?" I felt as if there were a boulder in my throat when I tried to answer, but I said, "I love you more than anything else in this world and I need you more than air."

For many months to follow, Millie's illness persisted. As parents, we battled our own sadness and frustration, turning to God daily so that our family's foundation of faith would not be shaken. There were days when Millie asked to change the tedium of laying in bed staring at a blank ceiling. I helped her to the living room sofa where she laid on her side and stared at the family carrying on with the day's business. I tried to keep family dinners as close to what they had been in hopes of giving my children a sense of security and stability. These regular family meals, however, sometimes served as a source of sadness for Millie because she could only participate from the couch while we were at the table. From her perspective, she saw what a motherless family looked like.

I encouraged her to remain strong and focused on recovery, so that Satan would not use our children's sadness as a conduit of disbelief. If we remained strong and grounded in faith, Satan was powerless. Millie agreed with me, so she used the images of family dinners without her as kindling for an internal fire. Millie burned with a new desire to live life—to continue home-schooling our two youngest children (even if this meant schooling them while she laid in bed), to reach out to our middle daughter who struggled in high school, and to stay in constant communication with our twin daughters while they were in college. From the bed in which Millie laid, she conducted family business and reclaimed her rightful position as referee/chef/taxidriver/cheerleader/butler/coach/banker.

Perfect Timing

"We won't be anxious, we'll cease our striving.
We'll wait on You because everyone knows that
*   You've got perfect timing*
And after Your testing comes Your blessings
Everyone knows that you have perfect timing."

Scott Underwood

By May 2002, Millie was well enough to attend Jasmine and Bianca's college graduation, and Alexandria's high school graduation. We were so proud of our daughters, but especially Alexandria because we saw such a positive change in her life. She reached out to Millie during her cancer and this relationship expedited Millie's recovery. Millie began walking on her own, speaking clearly and even began making dinner on a regular basis. It seemed as if the longer her red hair grew, the healthier she became. Millie was weaned off chemotherapy entirely by June 2002 and her doctors told her that everything appeared normal. Our family celebrated and thanked God for His continued mercy, grace and sovereignty through such a painful trial. But, little did we know that God would once again make our family retrace the fresh footprints left in the sands of time.

In December 2003, Millie struggled with her vision once again and her cancerous symptoms returned with a vengeance. Millie complained of extreme pain in her cranium where the shunt was placed, but for a few weeks the doctors couldn't identify the problem. Millie's brain surgeon discovered that her brain fluid wasn't circulating properly due to an infection surrounding the shunt and the valve that regulated the flow of cranial fluid. The same day this was discovered, Millie was rushed into emergency brain surgery to have the shunt relocated to other side of her brain. Everything happened so fast that we didn't have the opportunity to think about the consequences of this action. Millie and I quickly prayed and she was rushed into surgery.

I called my children to tell them what had happened and they met me at USC Medical Center. Because of the suddenness of Millie's diagnosis, I completely forgot that it was New Year's Eve. My children gathered together in the hospital lobby and we prayed that God would herald in the New Year with a new beginning for Millie.

Our prayers were honored when, in surgery, the doctor noticed that her brain was functioning without the help of the shunt and valve. He decided against replacing the shunt on the other side of her brain as planned. This was amazing news because the doctors initially told Millie that in 10 years she would need more brain surgery to replace the shunt. Our family was overjoyed with this development. By the grace of God, Millie's brain was functioning on its own—a true MIRACLE!!

Millie woke up at 9:30 p.m. to the sounds of my whispered prayers, heart monitors and oxygen. The nurses asked the visitors to leave, but before we did, I sneaked the kids into Millie's room wearing glittered hats and blowing party whistles to ring in the New Year. She smiled brightly and even managed to laugh. I remember looking at her and thinking how beautiful she looked when she smiled.

After kissing Millie goodnight, my kids and I went to *El Tepeyac Mexican Restaurant* in East Los Angeles. As usual, the food was delicious, but it tasted even better knowing that Millie was tucked away under hospital-issued sheets on her way to recovery. With melodic sounds of *Mariachi* music seeping from the beat-up juke box, we sat on mismatched chairs and prayed for our food, thanking God for giving us such an amazing mother and wife.

From that moment on, Millie's health has steadily been getting better. While some days are pockmarked with the side effects of cancer, we thank God every day for Millie's recovery and we know that He is going to use this experience to comfort others. In my eyes, Millie's journey proves that: (1) Prayer is powerful; (2)

the God we serve cares for us and listens to our cries; and (3) Jesus Christ, the Master Physician, heals and restores not only the body, but the soul.

Several years have passed since that New Year's Eve, but I continue to thank God for Millie's health, my family's progress and His awesome power. Although there were days when getting out of bed was the last thing I wanted to do, and crying behind closed doors was all I could do, God never let me hide underneath my covers. He dried my tears and never allowed Satan to shake the foundation of my faith.

I firmly believe that God put my family and me through the fire in order to prepare us for the ministry. By losing my home, losing my job, losing the ability to purchase a car, losing the capability to buy my children Christmas gifts, and almost losing my wife, God tested the inner parts of me. He has given me more than I could ever ask for: a growing church with devoted members of the body of Christ; an astoundingly beautiful and loving wife; and children who are actively walking with God and pursuing higher education. The blessings keep coming as my family continues to grow. In just a few weeks, my daughter, Jasmine, will be married in Hawaii.

133

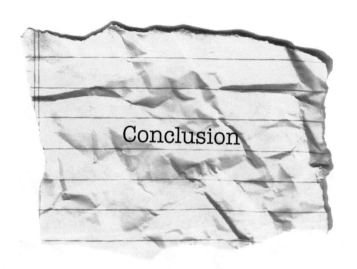

Conclusion

As I peruse the pages of this book before it goes to print, my daughter is still pestering me about finalizing her wedding plans. She goes on to remind me that this is a big day in her life and that she needs my full attention. Full attention! Her comment strikes a chord. For the entirety of her life, I have given Jasmine my utmost attention and catered to her every need. As her dad, I have tried my best to follow the example that Jesus has set forth for me. Jesus Christ cares for my every need and supports every step I take along the winding road called life.

At some point or another, I have held each one of my children in my arms when they fell off their bikes the same way the Lord has held me in His arms when I was in pain. I have comforted them during their darkest hours, the same way the Lord has comforted me. God willing, I will be by their side as they journey through life. In like manner, I know that the Lord will be by my side as I continue to follow His upward call.

Epilogue

Perhaps it was the Hawaiian shirt and the musky smell of Old Spice cologne that made me instantly attracted to him. No, wait, it must have been the way he worked the room with one broad sweep with his oversized personality. Like a moth, Pancho floated his way around the party and people were attracted to him the same way one might be attracted to a foreign animal exhibit at the zoo. People wanted to know what made Pancho so different, yet loveable.

Curiously, I was drawn to Pancho just like everyone else, although I tried my best to stay away from him. At first glance, I knew my parents wouldn't approve of his long hair (No daughter of ours is going to date a man with hair almost as long as hers!), of his background (Don't you know that Vietnam makes a man go crazy?!), or of his race (But, Millie, you know Mexicans and Puerto Ricans don't mix well). In spite of what my parents considered his faults, I loved Pancho with every bone in my body. He possessed the carefree personality that I longed for, the emotional depth that I lacked, and the uncanny ability to make me feel like I was the only girl in a crowded room.

To this day, Pancho still shares his personality and his charm not only with me, but from the pulpit. God has allowed my husband to use his past—both the good and the bad—to reach out to many people and I am in awe of the man the Lord has allowed him to become. I remember 35 years ago when Pancho and I went to Angelo's Restaurant in Alhambra after a party for late-night pizza. Back then, no one would have thought that the man passed-out next to me from drunkenness would ever become a pastor, but God can do amazing things with the lowly.

By the grace of God, Pancho has become an amazing husband and marvelous father. Though we struggled along in life and walked desolate roads, we struggled and walked together. There were times when we wanted to throw in the towel and give up on everything, but God never—never—let us down. During our darkest moments, the Lord always provided a light at the end of the proverbial tunnel. God destined Pancho to be my soul mate because, without him, I wouldn't have been able to walk the winding roads that I have traversed. When I battled brain cancer, Pancho was by my side every step of the way. Although the cancer was just as hard on him as it was on me, he found a way to pick up his cross and follow God's calling. Not only did Pancho wheel me into the hospital for my weekly chemotherapy treatments, he made it a point to stop by Krispy Kreme Donuts and buy a dozen for the nursing staff and doctors. When I finished my last cycle of chemotherapy, Pancho catered a Mexican meal—tacos, enchiladas, rice and beans—for the oncology ward at St. Jude Hospital. When the doctors thanked him, he replied that it was a small price to pay to see God work a miracle through their hands.

I know that God guided me to specific doctors in order to combat my cancer, but I also know that the true healing came from Jesus Christ. The entire congregation at Calvary Chapel Montebello rallied behind me with prayers and supplications. Their concern spilled over into other churches and I immediately became the recipient of cards, warm meals delivered to my doorstep, and much needed prayers. There was a time when I couldn't bear the idea of getting out of bed, much less going to church, but God spoke to me one Sunday evening when a young woman came up to me with a white piece of paper. I was feeling extremely ill and could hardly muster the strength to speak, but when she asked me to read what was neatly typed on the paper, I couldn't say no. It was the letterhead of a Baptist church in North Dakota and I couldn't figure out why this woman would want me to read something in my condition. After a quick glance, I realized that this paper was a prayer list that had been inserted into a church bulletin. On this prayer list—from a church I've never heard of, in a state I've never visited—my name was listed as well as my illnesses. This young woman went on to tell me that she visited the church while she was passing through North Dakota and, while she couldn't answer my questions as to how this church found out about my cancer, she wanted me to know there were many Christians praying for my healing. What an amazing God! I taped that prayer list to my refrigerator as a reminder that God was in control and He heard the prayers of His children.

It's been a few years since I have been treated for cancer, but I still suffer with health ailments. I ask God for a complete healing, but I know that He has things under control. My condition keeps Pancho and me close to the cross. The fragility of life keeps us tightly woven to each other and totally dependent on Jesus Christ. This dependence is marked by our constant belief that we are held tightly in God's arms. A few months ago, just as Pancho had big events planned for the church, I was stricken with Bells facial palsy. The left half my face had drooped and I had no control or feeling. On that Wednesday night, I walked into Pancho's office and we immediately knew that this was another test from God. I wanted to cry when Pancho held me in his arms, but he reminded me that we had been down this road before—we knew that we were being tested because God had big things in store for the church. To much is given, much is required and if my health is the price I have to pay for the upward calling of God, I will count the cost and continue to follow Him.

I have yet to be healed from the facial palsy, so I unabashedly use this opportunity to solicit prayers. Please pray for my health, but—more so—pray that God will use my sicknesses for the glory of His Kingdom.

It is my hope that this book is proof that God can use ordinary men to complete His Will. As I read through the pages of this book, I was taken back into our bittersweet past, but this has also caused me to look forward to a bright future. God has picked Pancho up from miry clay and molded him into a malleable man, ready and willing to do whatever it takes to show God how thankful he is for His undeserved salvation, redemption and justification. Please pray for the both of us as we try to follow the path God has laid out for our lives.

Acknowledgments

This book is a labor of love. I could not have pieced this project together without the help of many people and I am indebted to their kindness, patience and long-suffering.

Many thanks to Wendy Mukai for creating a cover that is reflective of my personality and roots—her artistic insight was invaluable throughout this process. When my words became knotted and mangled, my editor, Shiara Davila, untangled my thoughts and pieced them back together. I am appreciative for Carl Lawrence's feedback from the inception of this book— he provided the confidence I needed to keep going and pointed me in the right direction. This book would be nothing if it weren't for the eyes of Stephanie Arevalo, Hermann Garnica, Kevin Garnica, Sarah Garnica, and Jelani Solper proof-reading every copy again and again. Their hard work was especially appreciated as the book approached its deadline! Much appreciation to David Jay for taking time out of his schedule to bless me with *amazing* pictures of Jasmine and me— he's a wonderful photographer, but an even greater man. Thanks to Sean Lawrence—his knowledge and encouragement is the only reason this manuscript is where it is today. I am extraordinarily blessed because he took a grass-roots project and helped me form a book. A thousand times over, thanks.

Lastly, I need to thank my daughter, Jasmine, for sticking by my side throughout the course of this book. She is the catalyst for this project and it is because of her hard work and determination that I have been able to produce it. Together we took my memories, dressed them with words, and sent them falling onto blank pages—thank you, *mija*.